An Angel
Spoke to Me

An Angel
Spoke to Me

True Stories of Messages from Heaven

Theresa Cheung

**SIMON &
SCHUSTER**

London · New York · Sydney · Toronto

A CBS COMPANY

First published in Great Britain by Simon & Schuster UK Ltd, 2011
A CBS COMPANY

Copyright © 2011 by Theresa Cheung

1 3 5 7 9 10 8 6 4 2

Simon & Schuster UK Ltd
1st Floor
222 Gray's Inn Road
London WC1X 8HB

www.simonandschuster.co.uk

Simon & Schuster Australia
Sydney

A CIP catalogue record for this book is available
from the British Library.

ISBN: 978-1-84983-012-6

Typeset by M Rules

Printed in the UK by Cox & Wyman, Reading, Berkshire RG1 8EX

Contents

Acknowledgements

This book was a labour of love from start to finish and would simply not have been possible without the help and support of some amazing people. I especially want to thank my brilliant agent, Clare Hulton, for believing in and making this book happen; my wonderful editor, Kerri Sharp, for her insight and encouragement, and everyone at my fantastic publisher, Simon and Schuster, for being so very helpful throughout the entire process of writing this book and getting it ready for publication.

I'd also like to take this opportunity to sincerely thank everyone who has written to me over the years to share their inspiring angel stories, or to offer me their personal thoughts and insights. I'm deeply grateful to you all because your stories are the heart and soul of every angel book I write and I have no doubt that your words will bring hope and comfort to all those who read them.

Special thanks to Ray, Robert and Ruthie for their love and patience when I disappeared for hours on end to complete this project. And last, but by no means least, special thanks go to everyone who reads this book. I sincerely hope it will open your heart to the angel voices that can be heard all around you, and always within you.

We shall find peace.
We shall hear the angels,
We shall see the sky sparkling with diamonds.

Anton Chekhov

Introduction:
Words of Wonder

The quieter you become, the more you can hear.

Ram Dass

Yes, I believe in angels. I know they watch over me from above and speak to me on earth in countless different ways. I think we tend to dismiss a lot of incredible things that happen to us in our lives as mere chance, putting them down to coincidence or being in the right place at the right time, but if you have ever felt unexpected feelings of inspiration and love I believe this to be the voice of your guardian angel calling out to you. I also believe that celestial beings can talk to you through your dreams or through the spirits of departed loved ones. And sometimes they may choose to express themselves in the beauty and wonder of the natural world, or through other people who are consciously or unconsciously guided by those from the world of spirit.

Things haven't always had this clarity for me. Although I can't remember a time when I haven't been intrigued and enchanted by angels – because I was brought up in a family of psychics and spiritualists and talk of angels and spirits was the norm – I freely

admit there have been many times in my life when I have seriously questioned their existence. I'm sure I'm not alone here.
Perhaps you don't think you have ever heard heaven speak.
Perhaps you are drawn towards the idea of angels but don't think
you have seen or heard anything miraculous. Or perhaps you've
experienced something that you thought was out of this world at
the time it happened, but then doubted yourself and your experience afterwards.

How can you ever be really sure if you are hearing the voice
of an angel or not? This book is a collection of stories from ordinary people who have absolutely no doubt that an angel spoke
clearly and eloquently to them. All their accounts demonstrate
with refreshing honesty and clarity the many different ways
heaven can dip into our lives and change them for ever by healing wounds, mending or saving lives and filling them with a sense
of purpose, peace and love. It is my sincere wish that reading
these deeply personal and heartfelt accounts will open your mind
to the very real possibility that angels exist and that perhaps without realising it you may have already heard divine whispers. I
hope what you read will help remind you that there is so much
more to this life than you will ever know. I hope it will reassure
you that in our often troubled and conflicted world angels are
constantly sending us much needed messages of comfort, mercy,
goodness and eternal love from heaven.

For many years now I've been researching and writing about
angels and the afterlife experiences of people of all ages and back-
grounds, religions and walks of life. In that time I have not only
come to the firm understanding that beings of light exist, but also

to the realisation that everyone, whoever they are and wherever they come from, can if they open their heart and mind find their own unique and highly personal ways to see and hear the divine. I have also noticed that even though heavenly encounters can differ wildly in the details, and in the mediums the angels choose to manifest their loving presence, all of them are linked by the theme of heavenly helpers delivering messages, most typically messages of hope when all hope seems lost.

Looking back on my own life, I can see that this 'message of hope when all hope seems gone' theme has often been the case for me, and never more so than the bitterly cold winter of 1990, when life really didn't seem worth living any more.

All by myself

There was a time in my life, some twenty or so years ago now, when I felt utterly and completely alone. I'd felt lonely and abandoned before but never to the intense and soul-destroying degree I experienced back then. I still have my diary for that year and one entry date in particular, 25 December 1990, is a permanent reminder to me of just how bad things got. I've edited a lot of it down, because I wrote reams and reams, but here is some of it. I think you'll get the gist . . .

25 December 1990

Christmas Day and I'm all alone in the world. Mum's dead, my brother is travelling and I have no family, no partner, no one to call my own. I'm all alone on this 'happy day'. Everyone is waking up to presents and laughter but there's no reason for me even to get out of bed. It is so quiet. I can hear myself breathe. I do have friends, but I could never admit to them how lonely I feel. I would not want to burden them with that. Someone once said that loneliness is the worst form of poverty. They damn well got that right. I don't know what to do any more. I am not in love with my life at all. I am so miserable. Sometimes I wish this would all just end. I'm 25, and should be at the height of my powers, but don't feel my life has any value any more to anyone, not even to myself. My existence feels worse than death because death seems like a relief from loneliness. If there is an afterlife I will be with Mum and if there is nothing, well, at least it will be a relief from this curse of loneliness.

I hadn't planned to spend that Christmas Day all by myself. It just somehow ended up that way. I could have visited my brother but I didn't get along with his friends. I could have spent the day with a girlfriend but didn't want to feel like a charity case – besides, seeing her celebrating Christmas Day with her mum would have been overwhelming for me, as I was still raw from the loss of my mum. I could have done some volunteer work but just didn't have the motivation. I could have done many things that day, but instead I chose to do nothing because I knew that wherever I went and whoever I spent time with I would still feel utterly and completely alone.

I was fed up of never feeling truly understood; fed up of people not seeing the real me – they didn't even seem to try to see the real me. At times it felt like the real 'me' wasn't visible to anyone at all, and everyone had a different idea of who I was. I would spend time with people trying to connect but I felt they never ever got close to understanding me. I would feel so far away. The kind of loneliness I'm describing here is even lonelier than spending time alone. At least when I was alone I could feel like me, if that makes sense.

So there I was crying tears of loneliness and self-pity on Christmas Day. It was one of the most pitiful times in my life. When I was not crying physical tears I was crying tears of the spirit. I'm ashamed to admit that my thoughts did wander to death and whether it would be easier for me leave this world behind. It seemed so cruel to be born into a world crowded with people and not to feel connected, deeply connected to anyone living. I didn't think I could go on like this much longer and if my mother in spirit had appeared and offered to take me away I think I would gladly have followed her.

And that is how I knew I had reached rock bottom. I was in a self-created hell and I couldn't see a way out. When she was alive my mum often told me that heaven is a place you never want to leave and long to experience all your life, and so, I thought, hell must be a place where you always want to leave but never can. It's a place more dark and terrible than the nothingness of death. And for me all those years ago, the loneliness I was cursed with was such a place. It was like hell, always wanting to escape but never finding a way out. Worst of all my hell was inside me and wherever I went I would carry it with me. I felt trapped for all eternity.

I begged with every fibre of my being for a celestial being to come and save me. I did not know how to save myself. But no heavenly helper came. Nobody appeared. Nothing came to rescue me. Nobody came to sympathise or offer me hope. All that there seemed to be was me. I was completely alone. I was terrified. What I didn't realise at the time, but do understand now with the hindsight that age brings, is that being alone in life is one of those experiences – if we survive them – that can bring us into the core of our very being, knowing ourselves better than we ever have before.

With the world eerily silent on Christmas Day, I cried often and whiled away the long hours writing furiously in my journal. Sometimes it felt as if my hand could not keep up with the speed of my thoughts. There was, however, something compulsive but calming about pen and paper making contact. My thoughts were freed and my mind became more focused. Again, I did not realise it at the time but in the midst of my unhappiness, I was instinctively being drawn to the silent centre of my being. I think for the first time in my journal-writing life I started to be completely honest with myself. I felt there was nothing to gain from lying or pretending any more, and so I started to write down the kind of desperate stuff you read earlier. I felt like I was on a kind of spiritual quest. My soul was searching for truth. I had so many feelings to vent. I was in touch with myself. It was frightening facing 'me' like this but also strangely intoxicating. It was as if writing down my fears had begun the process of overcoming them.

Eventually fatigue took over and I drifted off to sleep. When I woke up I saw pages and pages of my untidy writing around my bed. Each page was filled with my thoughts, my inner screams and my pain. I tried reading some of it, and although most of it was incomprehensible, one word did seem to stand out clearly and consistently, and give my ramblings the illusion of order. It was the word 'angel'.

I don't know why but like a song you can't get out of your head I kept repeating the word angel in my mind. Then something made me sit down and transfer my thoughts to paper. I wrote the word 'angel'. I wrote it down again. Once I started I couldn't stop. I wrote it many times and each time I wrote it down I felt like something was lighting up inside me. It was as though I was writing it for the first time. There was something tremendous in it, something eternal, and something utterly compelling and mysterious, but also something light and familiar and important in my life. It was like remembering an incredible secret, one that I had forgotten but should not have.

It must have been five in the afternoon when I finally stopped writing. I could have gone on but my hands wouldn't let me. I was also incredibly thirsty so I left my bedroom to get a drink of water. Clumsy with hunger and eyes sore from crying, I knocked into my bookcase on the way out and a book fell onto the floor, hitting my foot. I reached down to pick it up and noticed that it was *The Diary of Anne Frank*. I had never actually read it from cover to cover, but had kept it because it was the last book my mum had read before she died. I still had the bookmark in the place where she had left it for the last time. It was full of Mum's characteristic page markings. She had a habit of underlining in pencil passages from books that spoke to her. I picked up the book and read that Anne called her diary Kitty. It was a gift, which she described as 'possibly the nicest of all', for her thirteenth birthday. It probably came to her at a moment when she needed it most.

Flicking through the book, my eyes settled on three passages that Mum had heavily underlined:

'I want to write, but more than that, I want to bring out all kinds of things that lie buried deep in . . . my heart . . . the reason for . . . my starting a diary: it is that I have no such real friend . . .

'Oh, so many things bubble up inside me as I lie in bed, having to put up with people I'm fed up with, who always misinterpret . . . my intentions. That's why in the end I always come back to . . . my diary. That is where I start and finish, because Kitty is always patient.

'I want to go on living after . . . my death! And therefore I am grateful to God for giving me this gift, this possibility of developing myself and of writing, of expressing all that is in me. I can shake off everything if I write; . . . My sorrows disappear . . . My courage is reborn.'

As I read these words of wonder my first instinct was shame. Here was I wallowing in self-pity and self-absorption but my situation was nothing compared to the hell that Anne Frank must have endured. At least I had choices. I could do something about my hell. Anne never had any choice. And it was this sudden and instant awareness that I really did have a choice that began to lift my darkness. Sure, I had not had an easy ride in life so far, but I wasn't a helpless victim as Anne had been. I had options.

I was quickly filled with a newfound sense of courage and awe. It was as if, through the words of Anne Frank, Mum was speaking to me from beyond the grave, giving me a sense of hope, purpose and direction. It was as if I was being given a nudge from the other side. It was all too much of a coincidence, the book falling down and me reading the passages just when I needed to read them the most. Trembling with excitement I had an overwhelming need for fresh air. I grabbed some clothes, gulped down some water and went outside.

Clutching my woollen cardigan tightly to keep myself warm, breathing in deep gasps of icy air, I sat on a bench beside the River Thames and for the first time since Mum died I didn't feel quite so alone. Yes, my day and much of my life so far had been agonisingly lonely but I wasn't as weak or as worthless as I had thought I was. Today, I had found the courage to face my deepest fears, and in the darkness I had found a flicker of light. I was a survivor. In my despair I had prayed for a miracle and out of love my guardian angel had spoken to me and given me a spark of hope and optimism again. I had been to hell but with the help of my angels I had found a way to transform it to heaven. I hadn't had a full-blown angel encounter, or sure-fire sign that my mum in spirit was watching over me, just a pen and paper and an open mind, but these had been enough to help me choose life instead of death.

This was by no means the end of my struggles and my self-doubts, and there have been many more challenges on my spiritual journey, but it was one of the first of many important psychic breakthroughs. I had a lot more to learn and a whole lot more growing up to do – and completely letting go of morbid self-absorption and feelings of isolation and separation from others was still a way off – but now at least I could see a way forward. I could see an end to my loneliness. It was gradually becoming clear to me that angels might very well be the key not just to my life, but to everything.

I'm in my mid-forties now and sometimes long to do a *Peggy Sue* and flit back in time to revisit my younger self. There is so much I would say to her. I would tell her that even when there seems no way out, there are always choices. I would tell her to make more mistakes and take more risks. I would tell her to not be afraid of opening up to others. I would tell her to laugh more. I would tell her that loneliness is simply a state of mind and in spirit we are never alone, but most of all I would tell her not to fear solitude. Being alone isn't a curse – it can be one of life's greatest joys. Don't get me wrong, spending times with loved ones is among my favourite things in the world, but I also know that solitude, the ability to spend time happily by yourself, is crucial for spiritual growth because it is only when you are alone that you can truly reach into yourself and find truth, beauty and soul. It is only when you are alone that you can speak honestly and intimately to the angel within yourself, and find answers to questions your mind can otherwise never manage to ask.

Finding moments of inner peace, love and joy is a starting point on the road to the divine and more often than not these moments can only be discovered in times of solitude and quiet reflection. I could have saved myself a whole lot of heartache if I had understood this earlier, but such insight tends to come with age and life experience. It doesn't have to be the school of hard knocks for everyone though. There are gentler paths to enlightenment.

For instance, all of us at some point in our lives will have heard or read words of incredible wisdom, be they in the form of poetry, religious texts, inspirational books or from a wise and insightful relative, friend or teacher. Sadly, the hustle and bustle of daily life often stops us from fully absorbing these words into our souls. It doesn't have to be that way though, if we can just pause for a while to reflect and let the words sink into our hearts, because our hearts will instantly recognise them to be words of wonder that can shoot through the dilemmas of our daily lives to the place where angels dwell.

For me, the well-known but forever current text below always has the feel of an open door to heaven. You've probably heard it before but I urge you to read it here again, preferably when you are by yourself; really give your heart a chance to drink it all in.

Desiderata

Go placidly amid the noise and haste, and remember what peace there may be in silence.

As far as possible, without surrender, be on good terms with all persons. Speak your truth quietly and clearly; and listen to others, even to the dull and the ignorant, they too have their story. Avoid loud and aggressive persons, they are vexations to the spirit.

If you compare yourself with others, you may become vain and bitter; for always there will be greater and lesser persons than yourself.

Enjoy your achievements as well as your plans. Keep interested in your own career, however humble; it is a real possession in the changing fortunes of time.

Exercise caution in your business affairs, for the world is full of trickery. But let this not blind you to what virtue there is; many persons strive for high ideals, and everywhere life is full of heroism. Be yourself. Especially, do not feign affection. Neither be cynical about love, for in the face of all aridity and disenchantment it is perennial as the grass.

Take kindly to the counsel of the years, gracefully surrendering the things of youth. Nurture strength of spirit to shield you in sudden misfortune. But do not distress yourself with imaginings. Many fears are born of fatigue and loneliness.

Beyond a wholesome discipline, be gentle with yourself. You are a child of the universe, no less than the trees and the stars; you have a right to be here. And whether or not it is clear to you, no doubt the universe is unfolding as it should.

Therefore be at peace with God, whatever you conceive Him to be, and whatever your labours and aspirations, in the noisy confusion of life, keep peace in your soul.

With all its sham, drudgery and broken dreams, it is still a beautiful world.

Be cheerful. Strive to be happy.

Max Ehrmann *c*.1920

I was first introduced to the *Desiderata* when I was sixteen. I was asked to read it out loud at a school assembly, but sadly at the time I wasn't ready to understand this heaven-sent opportunity.

My heart and my mind were just not ready. I needed to learn to get a handle on my nerves and grow in confidence and self-understanding first. After Christmas Day 1990, however, I have often found myself returning to it. Each time I read it I find something new to inspire and guide me and to remind me once again that when we are 'open' to angels, when we take a moment alone to pause and reflect and choose love and joy, all good things will come to us.

Perhaps you have some words of wonder that help you see the light, or help you feel protected and watched over or remind you that the forces of light will always be more powerful than the forces of darkness. If you don't think you have, perhaps this book will be like your pointer to heaven, a reminder of the enduring loving presence of angels in your life. Use it for strength, guidance and encouragement and whenever you feel alone. It is a beautiful world, but it can also be a painful, frightening and sometimes very lonely world. As the stories you read here will show you, it can be very inspiring to know that however tough your life gets your angels are always talking to you and sending you their messages of hope and love. They are always walking beside you, watching over you and waiting for you to open your heart and accept that they are on your side.

So accept that your angels are always within and around you. Accept that you are never alone. Believe that you can always hear their words of wonder. Allow their messages of comfort and hope to help you see the light. Let their whispers awaken your dreams. Let their voices give your spirit wings.

About angels

As an established angel author I'm often asked what an angel is. Typically, I'm reluctant to answer this profound question because in this life we can never fully know what they are, and every person will define angels in their own unique way, but for me an angel is a spiritual being that acts as a messenger between this world and the next. (The word angel actually means 'messenger' in Hebrew.) Angels exist both within and all around us whether we believe in them or not. They reveal themselves to the spiritual side of our nature, or as I like to call it the aspiring angel within each one of us, and from the moment we are born, perhaps even before, they are bound to us in ways we will never understand. It's possible they see us as children in need of support and guidance, but whatever the truth it is clear that they can speak to us both directly and indirectly, and sometimes they can intervene in our lives.

The traditional image of an angel is of a winged creature with flowing robes but I must stress that full-blown angel encounters of this kind are extremely rare. From my experience and research I have found that the form angels take will vary widely. They can choose to be visible or invisible. The possibilities for eternal goodness and love to manifest in this world are endless. To those with an open mind they can reveal their spiritual nature through coincidences, dreams, a sudden flash of intuition and the sensation of a magical loving presence around you. They can be found in the lyrics of a song, a hug, a smile or in anything or anyone that inspires or uplifts you. They can reveal themselves through any number of calling cards – white feathers, clouds, coins and rainbows being some of the most well known. Consciously or unconsciously they may also reveal themselves through other people, the natural world around us and last, but by no means least, the spirits of departed loved ones.

Many people think we become angels when we die. Strictly speaking this is a misunderstanding because angels are distinct kinds of spiritual beings that have never lived on earth, but from my research it is clear that angels can and do choose to manifest themselves through the spirits of departed loved ones.

I'm well aware that many people will find logical or psychological explanations for angel stories, but to those who have experienced them no amount of scepticism or explanation will ever have the power of their personal belief. (After all, isn't the definition of faith belief without the need for explanation or proof?) And to all those who doubt, or crave proof or evidence, I want to point to the hundreds of thousands of angel accounts that have been gathered over the centuries. The only logical conclusion for me, with so many trustworthy witness statements readily available, is that the angelic realm has always been and will always be all around us. There is a spiritual plane that intermingles with the physical world. People do not encounter angels because of their religion, their beliefs or even their desire or need; they meet them because the time is right for angels to make themselves known to them.

If desire or need, or the so-called right training or background, was a prerequisite for angel encounters then surely I, with my spiritualist upbringing, should have heard the voices of angels from an early age? This couldn't have been further from the truth. When I was growing up in a household of psychics I often felt frustrated and inadequate because I hadn't inherited the gift. I longed to see angels like my mother could. I attended many psychic development workshops and classes where fellow students could hear divine voices and see visions of heavenly beauty. I just sat in darkness, seeing and hearing nothing. Although there were glimmers of hope along the way, it wasn't really until I was in my late thirties/early forties that these channels gradually began to open up for me.

I've made huge progress but even today, much as I would like to, I still can't see or hear angels like a seasoned psychic can. Somehow though this doesn't matter to me any more, because I have finally learned that, like everyone else, I can and do hear angels in my own unique way. And looking back on my life I have also learned that all along they were speaking to me, I was just too full of fear and self-doubt to listen. Fear and self-doubt are natural predators of the angels.

It is a hugely encouraging sign today that ever-increasing numbers of people are moving beyond their fears and self-doubts and welcoming angels into their hearts and their lives. It seems that our divine helpers are revealing themselves as never before. Angels really do seem to be all around. There are countless sites on the internet devoted to them and countless books as well as magazines, newsletters and memorabilia. The very fact that I am writing this book is a fantastic sign because five or ten years ago publishers would never have thought that there would be the readership out there, but with several of my books charting in the top ten of the *Sunday Times* bestsellers list in recent years, it is clear that angels are being taken into people's homes and hearts all over the world.

Even though angels seem to be emerging everywhere these days, it is a sad reality that poverty, violence, injustice, pain, misfortune, suffering and natural and man-made disasters also seem to be everywhere. I'm constantly being asked why, if angels exist, they allow all this to continue. How they can let an innocent child starve to death and a murderer escape justice? How they can save one life and not another? Where were our angels on 9/11 and 7/7?

I find such cruel injustices as hard to understand and accept as anyone else, but I have come to accept that there are some things in this life we will never understand until we pass to the other side and can see the bigger picture. I don't claim to know the answers to those big 'why' questions, but one thing I do know and that is this: we need our heavenly helpers as never before. It is critical now for us to believe in the love and goodness that exists in and around us and it is critical for us to trust that this love and goodness will always be stronger than the forces of darkness, pain and helplessness in the world. That's why there can be no better time for this book to be published so yet another voice can join the ever-increasing chorus of those who believe in angels.

About this book

Ever since I first started writing about the psychic world – which is some twenty or so years now – I have been astonished and delighted by the vast number of communications I have received about angels and spirits via letter, and now most typically by email, from people around the world. It is a privilege and an honour for me to be able to gather these stories together and share them with a wide readership. Punctuated with my own experiences and insights you'll find a selection of these amazing stories here in this book. In some cases names and details have been changed to protect identity, or edited down for clarity, but all the people who were generous enough to contribute their stories touched me greatly with their truth and honesty, and I have no reason to doubt their integrity.

Like me, the people whose stories you will read here are not mediums, psychics or 'new agers', but ordinary people leading ordinary lives. Some of them believed in angels before their experience but others did not and would even have scoffed at the very idea before heaven dipped into their lives and transformed everything. Some of them were religious, but many more were not. Like increasing numbers of people today they believed in something but were not sure what. All this has confirmed my conviction that in an increasingly divided world angels are a much needed uniting force that can cut across all creeds, religions, cultures and belief systems.

The focus of this book is the way that angels speak to us from heaven. Because of space limitations I wasn't able to include every story I wanted to – so apologies if you have sent me a story and it isn't included here; perhaps next time – but I hope the accounts that you find here will give you a full and radiant picture of the many different ways messages can be sent from heaven. I hope you will find the stories as profound and inspiring as they never fail to be for me. But before I share these true stories with you, as I always do in my books, in chapter one I'd like to share some more of my spiritual journey with you. I'm hoping this will help you get to know me better and also underline heavily my point that, like most of the people who contributed their stories to this book, I'm an ordinary person with no special psychic or mediumistic powers, but this hasn't stopped magical things happening to me.

Finally, before you plunge in I'd just like to thank you for picking up this book and joining the growing numbers of people around the world who long to hear the voices of angels in their everyday lives. As you read, may you recognise yourself in these stories many, many times over.

May you wake up one day and hear angels calling your name.

CHAPTER 1

Angels Calling My Name

Knowing yourself is the beginning of all wisdom.
Aristotle

'You're just too sensitive for your own good.'

'You've really got to toughen up.'

'Stop being such a cry-baby.'

'Scaredy-cat.'

I heard this said a lot to me when I was growing up. It always made me feel like there was something very weak and inadequate about me. I was convinced that I had a fatal flaw and that I had to hide it as best I could. I believed there was something wrong with me.

One memory stands out in particular. I must have been about nine years old at the time and I was on the bus to school. I was feeling very pleased with myself because I had finally mustered up the courage to climb the stairs and get a seat upstairs, but I didn't have just any seat, I had the front seat. It felt wonderful seeing the world from such a height. I felt invincible. Then in an instant my elation and sense of freedom turned to trauma as a bird smacked into the window and then slid down the pane and under the wheels of the bus.

A couple of boys sitting in the seat next to me found the whole thing very exciting, but the violent end of that bird seemed to penetrate far into my being. Tears filled my eyes and the laughter and chatter of the boys was intolerable. I heard one of them say that the bird was probably stuck to the wheels of the bus going round and round. Another said that it was probably wandering about beside the road with its head on back to front. The rest of the journey to school was pure torment for me as, seeing my distress, the boys took great delight in discussing every gruesome possibility. Fighting back tears, I couldn't concentrate at school for thinking about what might have happened to the bird.

After school on the way home I sat downstairs on the bus, hardly daring to look out of the window, but unable to stop myself. When the bus got close to the spot where the bird had hit the window, I looked out and saw it lying in a heap of red feathers on the side of the road. It was like an arrow to my heart. Tears drenched my face. For the next few days, weeks even, I could not tear my thoughts away from the suffering and lonely death of that bird. For the next year I wouldn't ride on the upper deck of a bus.

This incident wasn't an isolated one. At school I was often teased for crying or overreacting to things. If I didn't understand something the teacher was trying to tell me, my eyes would well up. If friends didn't want to play with me I would blubber. I would over-analyse everything that was said to me. Small wonder really that I didn't have many friends as a child. It must have been like walking on eggshells for them. At night my mum would hold me in her arms as I sobbed out my hurt feelings. She would tell me over and over again that I needed to stop taking everything so personally. She tried to teach me simple calming meditation exercises, like imagining a protective bubble around me, but nothing worked. I couldn't distance myself from anyone or anything.

Not surprisingly given my nervous disposition, fitting in was an issue when I was growing up in the loud and colourful 1970s. I was painfully shy. I remember many an excruciating school lunchtime clutching my blue plastic tray and wondering if anyone would let me sit by them. I remember many a painful PE session when team leaders picked everyone but me for their team. I remember many an anxious lesson sitting on a table by myself and many a fearful playtime hiding away from the fun.

My family's alternative lifestyle didn't help matters much when it came to fitting in. You see, I grew up in a family of psychics and spiritualists and nobody really understood what all that was about. Mum earned her living as a psychic counsellor, which basically meant that we had very little money and lived a gypsy-like lifestyle, forever on the move. We never seemed to settle in one place long enough to call it home, so even if I did start making a friend or two soon it was time for us to move and I had to start all over again. And then things took another turn for the worse when my parents separated. I'd never had a close relationship with my father, but when he left us a part of me felt even more rejected and isolated.

As a teenager my sensitivity just deepened. Bright lights, loud noises, strong smells and crowds had now become exhausting and overwhelming ordeals for me. I also developed an intense craving for solitude. Time alone to regroup after any kind of stimulation was as essential for me as food and drink. Like a character in a Jane Austen novel I needed periods of reflection and withdrawal. Hardest of all to deal with, though, was my habit of breaking into spontaneous tears and my tendency to run away from situations that made me feel exposed. To give just one of many examples, I remember being at the dentist's surgery once for a check-up. I must have been about fifteen at the time. I was thirsty and went to the water cooler for a drink. I grabbed a cup and just as I did my name was called out. Stressed, I pulled the water lever down without putting the cup in position and water splashed all over the floor. Everybody in the surgery was looking at me and I was mortified. Tears stinging my eyes, I could only think of one thing, leaving instantly. I grabbed my bag and ran out immediately, missing my appointment.

Being sensitive to large numbers of people, life at a huge and under-performing girls' comprehensive school was pure torture for me, so I left as soon as I could at the age of sixteen with a very poor set of qualifications. It's not that I was lazy, unable or didn't want to learn, I just couldn't concentrate in class. There was always so much noise and distraction. My end-of-school report was dismal. My school had clearly given up on me and didn't see much future ahead. I still wanted to learn though so I got a weekend job as a care assistant in an old people's home to help

Mum with the finances and carried on with my A-level education at home via a correspondence course.

You might think this was a bizarre lifestyle choice for a young
girl, and plenty of people told me I was being ridiculous and
would need therapy sooner or later, but it worked for me. The
nursing home was quiet, and now Dad and Mum had separated
and my brother was at college, life at home with Mum was very
quiet and conducive to studying. So, for the next two years, apart
from Mum and a handful of elderly residents, I didn't really have
much to do with anyone. My teenage years were unusual to say
the least.

And all that quiet time paid off because much to my surprise –
and the shock of my former schoolteachers – I gained the
necessary results for a place at Cambridge University, reading
Theology and English. Sure, there were jubilations, but as time
wore on my anxieties returned. How was I ever going to fit in?
Although I loved being a university student, it was obvious very
early on that I was never going to belong there either. I just
didn't have the financial background or social connections and
'know-how' to keep up with the privately educated and, in those
days, male-dominated 'elite' I found myself thrown in with. In
short, I was once again the complete outsider, the square peg in
a round hole.

At times, I felt like the university's social experiment. I
remember often locking myself in my room, terrified of going
into the magnificent dining hall. It was just too overwhelming
and I didn't feel I had any right to be there. Instead I would sit
in my room with a packet of crisps and a bottle of water, only

venturing out when I had lectures or tutorials to attend. I didn't join in with university social life at all. It wasn't that I didn't want to. It was simply that I didn't know how. I remembered all those times at junior school the other children had called me weird. I had taken all their taunting personally and deep down was convinced that nobody liked me. I would never belong. I was the social outcast. I kept this up for three years, failing even to attend my graduation. I got my degree but I was the invisible student.

With such low levels of confidence I was woefully ill equipped to deal with life in the real world. I was an accident waiting to happen and made some terrible career and relationship choices when I left university. Instead of using my degree to get job satisfaction, my low self-esteem stopped me applying for jobs that suited me. Instead of going out with men who treated me as an equal, I went out with men who used and abused me because I didn't think I deserved any better. This nomadic, confused and rather sad existence went on for several years. Sometimes it really did feel as if I couldn't cope with everyday life. My best and only friend was my mum, which meant that the pain of losing her to cancer when I was in my mid-twenties was unbearable. My life was broken and my heart was broken.

I could go on and on with anecdotes like this. I always hoped that one day – when I was a real grown-up – I would leave my hypersensitivity behind along with my childhood. I would grow out of my shyness. However, by my late twenties, I still didn't feel confident or have any sense of belonging in the world around me. Getting older did bring some improvements. I started to gather a few friends around me for one thing. I typically found myself in the role of listener and it suited me fine. My willingness to hear what others had to say, and not interrupt with my own life story, my ability to adapt myself to whatever the situation required and be as pleasing and as helpful as I possibly could for others was a 'winning formula'. I just didn't talk about myself. A lot of people liked me for that and it wasn't all one-way traffic, I liked the way giving to and helping others made me feel.

Another small step in the right direction was that I gradually began to understand myself better. With my deep reactions to feelings, nature, art and music and a strong need for personal freedom I realised that an office-bound job wasn't for me. I started work as a freelance journalist and writer and discovered a work satisfaction I have never known before. I also discovered a passion for informing, teaching and healing others through my writing. However, despite this drive to help others I still felt different from other people, as if I was from an alien planet. I wrote articles and books about leading a healthy, happy life, but there I was struggling with weight issues, relationship issues and low self-esteem. I was the cliché of the wounded healer.

So, I guess you could say I limped along and found ways to disguise my hypersensitivity and feelings of inadequacy. My angels must have been looking out for me, though, because against all odds I did somehow manage to land on my feet and eventually find a good man. I was also blessed with two beautiful children. There were bouts of postnatal depression after the birth of both my children, but I never fell completely into the darkness, and the deep and very real love I had for my children always helped me keep my head above water.

Indeed, it wasn't when my children were babies that I felt at my most vulnerable. I was in my mid-thirties and my young children were ready to spend time outside of the home mixing with other kids. Once again my fears made this normal rite of passage a time of great anxiety, but mercifully for me and my children my angels showed me a positive way forward. Unaware at the time that heaven was helping me, I was at a crossroads in my life where I would learn the important lesson of 'letting go', and accepting and embracing who I was. Along the way, I also finally discovered a deep and lasting sense of belonging and purpose. And here's how it happened.

Letting go

When I first had to leave my children at daycare a part of me withered and died. After so many months of being joined to them at the hip I had to try to rebuild my life. I always knew the day would come but it came all too quickly. I had felt safe at home alone with my children, and venturing outside into the world again seemed terrifying. At home I had done all I could to ensure family life was quiet and ordered. I was inseparable from my children, sensing their every need. However, when the nursery deadline loomed on the horizon I turned to jelly. All that love, attention, energy and time I had poured into my children and now I had to hand them over to someone else.

To make matters worse my son was quite a clingy child, anxious and tearful even when I left the room. How was I going to send him to school? On the first day a nursery nurse told me not to do any long goodbyes and simply head out the door. I did as I was told and retreated hastily, but then I heard the familiar wailing of my son. I rushed back inside and saw him being whisked away by a very capable-looking nursery nurse. The manager on duty said he would soon settle and if there were any problems she would give me a call.

I went back to my car and started weeping hysterically. My head was all over the place. Instead of using the time productively, I just sat in the nursery car park. I had to be near my children. After half an hour I called the nursery to see how things were going. I was told that my son was still crying but not as violently and my daughter was sleeping. The girl on the phone was so matter-of-fact in her description it really got to me. Didn't she understand what I was going through?

For the next three hours I sat in the nursery car park. There was no other place I felt I could be. I clutched my mobile in my hand, willing it to ring so I could go in and pick up my kids. The call didn't come and so I waited and waited. Eventually it was midday and I went back inside. My children were brought out to me and immediately I sensed how unsettled they felt. My son rushed up to me and grabbed me so strongly that I almost toppled over. My daughter was handed to me and I noticed that she had food stains around her mouth.

Later that evening I couldn't bring myself to tell my husband about sitting in the nursery car park for three hours. It sounded so pathetic. I did, however, tell him that I thought the standard of care at the nursery was poor and I was going to find another one. I didn't feel good about this as there was nothing wrong with the nursery, but I needed an excuse. I just wasn't ready to let my children go yet. So, for the next year or so I hired au pairs to come and sit with my children in my house while I worked. It wasn't ideal, and I didn't get much work done at all, but it did enable me to at least take on some jobs and gradually start earning again.

Time flew by quickly and before long my son was due to start school. Having felt so alienated at school myself, you can imagine how I felt about sending my son there. I wanted to home educate him but my husband put his foot down and said that wasn't going to happen. Unlike me, he had fond memories of his school days and he believed it was time for me to start letting go.

Letting go sounds so easy, but like many things in my life, what should have been easy was once again incredibly hard. I cried my heart out when I waved goodbye to him at the school gates. I didn't even make it to the car. The other mums gathered around me, concerned, and it was the oddest sensation for me as I was usually the one doing the comforting, the listening. Looking back, I think all of them felt like I did to some extent. They were just better at hiding it than I was.

Eventually, I dried my eyes and tried unsuccessfully to get on with my day. When it was time for pick-up I arrived a good half an hour early. Finally, the school bell rang and the children bustled out of the building. I stood anxiously on tiptoes craning my neck to see my son, but he didn't come out with the kids I thought were in his class. Once again my heart started racing. This was my worst possible fear. Something terrible had happened to my son.

Panicking, I ran into the school and started shouting his name. There wasn't any answer. I went outside again and there he was. He was sitting on the floor with another boy, both staring intently at the ground. Sweating profusely, I rushed to him and grabbed him but he struggled to get away as he was eager to get back to his game. The other boy's mum came over to me and told me that my son and her son had come out of school together with one mission – to find ants. She apologised for not seeking me out sooner, but they seemed to be having so much fun. I took a few steps back to compose myself and fan my hot cheeks with my hands.

At that moment an older lady – I assumed she was the grand-mother of my son's new friend because she looked so much like his mother – came over to me and gave me a reassuring pat on the shoulder. 'It's OK,' she said. 'It's not that he doesn't want to be with you. He was just having fun with his new friend.'

Something about this woman, her warm and gentle manner, calmed me down instantly. I smiled at her and told her it was his first real time away from home and it was difficult for me. She smiled and, although I may not have her exact words right because, bear with me, I'm working from memories here, she said something along the lines of: '*I'm going to tell you something I told my daughter when she felt sad taking her children to school. Children are loaned to us for eighteen years so we can help them learn to fly. Being a parent is all about letting go of them gently. It begins with the cutting of the umbilical cord, the end of breastfeeding, their first steps and with each passing year we lose just a little bit more. From the moment they are born our job as mothers is to teach them little by little*

11

to fly on their own, because we are the way they learn to be successful, independent and fulfilled. However, even though they may fly far away from you, you can always be connected to them through love. This new connection can last for eternity when you understand that your child is always part of you and here with you.'

There are moments in your life when you know you are hearing something profound and deeply significant and this was one of those moments. I turned around to look at my son and as I did he looked up and smiled happily at me before returning to his ant-hunting game. I turned back to talk to the woman again, but she was gone.

By now the other boy's mother had come over and I asked her where her mother had gone. She gave me the oddest look and told me her mother had passed on just a few months ago. Her eyes reddened as she explained how happy this first day of school would have made her mother and how sad it was that she wasn't here to see it. Without hesitating, I told this woman about my conversation with the woman that I thought had been her mother because of the resemblance. When I had finished she stared at me for several moments and told me that she recalled her mother giving her the exact same advice about children being on loan to us from heaven, when her eldest child first started school two years ago and she was feeling anxious and unsettled.

It was a remarkable moment for us both. And for me it was the beginning of a much more confident and fulfilling phase of my life as a mother. This doesn't mean I haven't stopped worrying about my children – feeling guilty and worried is second nature to every mother whatever age her children are – but bit by bit I have understood the importance of letting go. I realised that keeping my children so close to me was a suffocating kind of love and I want to give them the best kind of love – the love that gives them wings. I don't want them growing up feeling insecure, helpless and vulnerable, and the best way to help them grow in confidence, self-belief and independence is to let them know I trust them and believe they can cope without me. I have learned to accept that they don't belong to me. Just as that lady at the gates told me, like everything wonderful in our lives, they are gift.

Do I think that the grandmother I spoke to at the gates was an angel? In the seven years since my kids have been attending that school I have never seen her again so she could well have been, but it could also have been a remarkable coincidence: a wise lady passing by who saw my distress and offered her words of wisdom at just the right time. Either way that lady was a message sent from heaven to me because she had such a positive impact on my life and the lives of my children. I can truthfully say that from that day forward I was a more contented mum. I was also a happier and more fulfilled person in general. I'm jumping ahead of myself here, so let me rewind and explain.

Coming home

As you've seen, feeling isolated and different because of my anxieties and fears felt like a heavy curse, but after learning to cope with my separation anxiety concerning my children, I was finally able to fully immerse myself in my writing while they were at school. Before, my head hadn't really been in the right place and I couldn't concentrate for worry, but now it didn't feel like a betrayal of my children to give over a part of myself to my work.

With renewed enthusiasm and passion I put my pen, or should I say keyboard, where my heart was and made the decision to do something with all the angel stories I had gathered over the years as a paranormal writer and researcher. The material was so personal and so life-transforming that in my mind's eye I could clearly see these stories gathered together in book form and it was time to stop hesitating and start doing something about it. My experience at the school gate – and the very real possibility that I had encountered something paranormal – felt like yet another prod from the world of spirit. It was time for me to make a commitment. Looking back on my life, I had had other remarkable encounters and experiences like this and, in an increasingly sceptical and material world, I needed to emerge from my hiding place and finally come clean about my encounters with, and belief in, the world of spirit.

Although today I openly write about angels I need to point out that seven or so years ago this wasn't yet the case. I was still in the process of establishing myself as a writer and most of my books were in the field of health, education and popular psychology. I was also working on a number of fairly heavyweight academic-style encyclopaedias. Until then I had always felt that to retain the respect of the academic community that had nurtured my inquisitive mind, I had to be low-key and objective about my devotion to the world of spirit. To be honest, I think a part of me was embarrassed about my spiritualist upbringing, so desperate was I to belong and fit in. However, after my school-gate angel encounter, as I like to call it, all that changed. I finally stopped trying to fit in and found the courage to stand by my beliefs. I was losing my objectivity, and standing out rather than blending in, but I was gaining a sense of purpose and meaning.

Taken in isolation I could perhaps have dismissed as coincidence, or explained away logically, certain extraordinary things that had happened to me in my life, but not when I began to put them all together and started to look at the bigger picture. For example, when my son was eight months old, did an angel appear in the guise of a ten-year-old boy who saved him from falling down some stone steps and then miraculously disappeared? After the birth of my daughter did a series of divine signs and a lucid dream rescue me from the darkness of postnatal depression? After the death of my father did he visit me in spirit and heal the wounds between us?

There had been so many incidents in my life when the veil between this world and the next seemed to vanish. And now I could at last see, with a clarity I had never known before, that all along my angels had been speaking to me, just not in the way I had expected. They had always been around, protecting and guiding me. I just hadn't been ready to hear their voices, or see them for what they really were.

In the next few years as I began to write up my experiences and gather angel stories from others and eventually turn them into bestselling books, further stunning coincidences, lucid and profound dreams and other miraculous encounters continued to occur, as if to reinforce to me the reality of angels and spirits and their very real presence in my life and the lives of others. In the process, I also unearthed another astonishing and life-changing truth, something I had also not been able to recognise before. As people got in touch with me to send in their stories and talk about their experiences and beliefs, it dawned on me that many of them seemed to display similar personality traits to mine.

Many of them told me that they were also highly sensitive and attuned to the feelings of others or the environment they were in. They abhorred violence in any form and felt a deep connection with beauty, nature and animals. For some, just reading distressing newspaper reports, or watching them on the TV, was enough to plunge them into the depths of despair, so deep was their empathy for the suffering of others. Many felt they had a passion for healing, helping or teaching others even though in their own lives they often struggled with self-esteem or relationship challenges, weight issues and the like, and didn't know how to translate this passion into a reality. Some talked about being miserable at school and always feeling different, as if dropped off from another planet.

The great majority didn't claim to be psychic, or even to have had a full-blown angel sighting complete with wings and halo, but they still believed that what they had experienced in their lives was extraordinary. They believed in something but they didn't know what that something was. Reading these wonderful people's stories and insights was like looking into my own heart, my own soul. I wasn't alone at all. For the first time in my life I felt like I belonged. I was coming home.

I started to do some of my own research and along the way

stumbled across – or perhaps I was guided to – a term I hadn't come across before: the 'highly sensitive person'. The so-called highly sensitive person is someone whose nervous system is so acutely attuned to the environment they are in, or the people they are with, that they process information very deeply and are easily upset by insensitivity or violence of any kind. Loud noises, crowds, busy streets, stress and even powerful aromas can provide too much stimulation. The incidence of stress and depression is higher than normal among such people because they are easily overwhelmed by the world around them, often tending to shut down or withdraw. Then they wonder what is wrong with them, why they can't get on with everyday routines and challenges like everyone else.

Curious to learn more because of the strong sense of famil-iarity I was experiencing, I found out that as many as one in five people could test positive for high sensitivity. This innate sensi-tivity has been well researched and the term Highly Sensitive Person was first coined in 1996 by Elaine N. Aron, Ph.D, who believed it was actually a genetic trait. In times past, people with high degrees of sensitivity to the world around them and within them may have become shamen, healers or counsellors, mediat-ing conflicts or bridging the gap between this world and the next. However, in today's increasingly secular world the appreciation of people with high levels of sensitivity has all but disappeared. In fact, they may often be considered odd, anti-social or 'out of it'. Many are constantly told that they are too sensitive, that they need to get thicker skin or come out of themselves or, worse still, that something is wrong with them.

The more I read about the highly sensitive personality, the more I began to recognise many of my own struggles and experiences, along with the struggles, insights and stories of the people writing to me.

Digging deeper I also discovered that psychologists believe highly sensitive people can't change their natures, and shouldn't have too. There are many amazing traits that come with being sensitive, including a high degree of imagination and creativity, a love of peace and calm, as well as empathy and compassion for people and animals, an intuitive approach to life and an idealistic view of just how beautiful the world could be. Most significantly, though, sensitive-natured people tend to have a deep connection or fascination with the spirit world. They may not always be able to articulate it, but they have a strong belief that a spiritual force is at work in their lives. Indeed, for the highly sensitive it could be said that developing spiritually is essential for their fulfilment and happiness.

How I wished I had had access to this kind of insight and information before. How it would have helped me deal with my sensitivity and feelings of alienation when I was growing up. Just knowing that I wasn't alone, and that what I had been regarding as my weaknesses could be turned into my greatest strength, was incredibly reassuring and comforting.

And this is when I had a light-bulb moment. Realising it was crucially important for sensitive people to develop spiritually, because if they didn't they could get easily hurt and disillusioned, I made it my mission to gather angel stories and share them with as wide a readership as I could. I didn't want anyone to feel as isolated and out of touch as I did. All those people sending me their stories and searching for deeper meaning in their lives, they were the angels calling my name.

With ever-increasing numbers of people believing in angels – either because they have personal experience of them or because they are in tune with the message of peace, love, beauty and hope angels bring – it is my sincere hope that there will be a wider acceptance of those with a more sensitive nature. Instead of trying to change, or berating themselves for being too shy or sensitive or spiritually inclined in a material world, after reading my books these people will know they are not alone, and hopefully this knowledge will help them find the confidence to appreciate and develop their unique traits, instead of trying to deny or repress them.

In a world fraught with violence, noise, chaos and increasing pressure to do everything faster and to have more and more material possessions, I believe sensitive souls are needed by society more than ever. Indeed, their stories and experiences point the way forward for everyone, inspiring others also to look within and discover the spiritual forces behind their lives.

In short, *you* – and your desire for a more magical, loving and peaceful world where angels and spirits can be seen, felt and heard – are needed now more than ever. You may wonder how I can say this about you. How can I tell that you have a sensitive soul, or that there is an aspiring angel inside you? I can tell because somehow this book found its way into your hands. Quite amazing really, when you think of the millions of other books, e-books, magazines, newspapers, and so on you could be reading out there. I am in no doubt that either the angels around you, or the aspiring angel inside you, guided you towards it. You were meant to read it.

And when you let your angels guide you in this way, you become the divine word the world is longing to hear. Through you others can hear the voice of an angel and catch a glimpse of heaven on earth. It goes right past their doubts and their fears and silently slips into their hearts. Then one day that voice will echo from deep within and speak to them, just as it is speaking to you now.

Guided by love

Whether you believe you have encountered angels or not in your life, the fact that you are drawn to the idea of them is an expression of your essential goodness and divinity. Sure, it is not always possible to stay on the right path. All of us will stray into weakness at some point in our lives or make the wrong choices, but that spark of essential goodness within us will never completely go out; if we can make the choice to follow it, however far we have strayed away, it will always take us back into the light.

I've strayed from the light many times during my life and haven't always trusted my angels, but now at long last as I approach my forty-sixth birthday, I do feel their presence every day. I have experienced enough myself and read enough about other people's experiences to know that they are always here with me, but personal experience and gathering stories from other people aren't the real reasons I believe in angels. I believe in them – and no longer have the intense need for 'proof' that I used to crave when I was growing up – not because of what I have experienced, been taught or read, but because deep down I believe in – and probably have always believed in – the all-conquering power of love. Love is the only language that angels speak. Love is the key through this life and the next.

It can be sometimes be hard to understand that love really is the key to eternal life, especially if you have suffered pain or experienced hatred, injustice and anger, but the only true and lasting way out of the darkness is love without expecting anything in return. There is no guarantee that others will love you as you would want to be loved, because love is always a choice, but I can guarantee that the love you choose to give freely will always return to live inside your heart. For in the love you give to others, lies the seed of heaven. Love has the power to transform the hell of suffering into heaven.

Angels are given to us from birth. They are here to guide and protect us through life. Whether we believe in them or not, they are there anyway. But the more we know about them, the more we think about them, the more likely we are to notice and recognise them when we do encounter them. I hope and trust, then, that the remaining chapters in this book will teach you a great deal more about angels, so that the next time one crosses your path or gently knocks from within your heart, you will instantly know that a beautiful and loving celestial being is calling your name, urging you to be stronger, deeper and so much more powerful than you ever thought you could be.

I hope and trust that from now on you will hear the voices of angels guiding you through this life and the next with their love.

And now I will show you the most excellent way.

If I speak in the tongues of men and of angels, but have not love, I am only a resounding gong or a clanging cymbal. If I have the gift of prophecy and can fathom all mysteries and all knowledge, and if I have a faith that can move mountains, but have not love, I am nothing. If I give all I possess to the poor and surrender my body to the flames, but have not love, I gain nothing.

Love is patient, love is kind and is not jealous; love does not brag and is not arrogant, does not act unbecomingly; it does not seek its own, is not provoked, does not take into account a wrong suffered, does not rejoice in unrighteousness, but rejoices with the truth; bears all things, believes all things, hopes all things, endures all things.

Love never fails . . . But now faith, hope, love, abide these three; but the greatest of these is love.

1 Corinthians 13:4-7,13

And just before you move on, if you do have any angel stories yourself I urge you to share them with other people or with me – details about how to do this can be found at the end of this book. Remember, angel voices can be heard in many different ways and they are most likely to be heard in ways you don't expect or aren't ready to understand at the time. The lady I met at the school gates didn't look or sound like an angel to me, but with hindsight I can see that this is exactly what she was to me at the time.

If you aren't sure whether you have heard divine voices, don't trust your head – there is often too much fear and doubt there – trust your heart, and have the courage to dream, for what you dream can become your life. And if you are scared of opening your heart because you fear it might be broken or disappointed, remember it is always better to have your heart broken than to try to escape heartache with all your might. A broken heart can be reborn, but a heart engaged in battle cannot die nor live nor know the wonder and beauty of love at all.

Learn to listen to your inner voice. Listen to your heart. It's your connection to spirit, to people, to the universe, and to yourself. The journey of a thousand miles begins with one step. The journey to your angels always begins with your heart.

CHAPTER 2

Celestial Voices

Angels are sent to bring us messages from God's heart.

Charles Hunter

Hearing voices is often considered to be the first sign of madness. I must admit that when I first considered writing a book with the title *An Angel Spoke to Me*, I did feel apprehensive. I've spent the greater part of the last ten years trying to convince people that there is nothing insane about seeing or hearing angels, nothing verging on what many might call the 'loony' fringe. But here I am talking about people who believe they can hear the voice of spirit, and discussing my own experiences of angel communications. I do hope, however, that the accounts you read here from normal people with normal lives will show you that hearing divine voices is perhaps the sanest, and most honest, loving and logical sound you will ever hear in the face of a world that appears to grow more confusing, illogical, unjust, chaotic and insane by the day.

Many of the world's greatest artists, inventors, and saints have received divine inspiration or guidance through hearing voices, but it's not just geniuses that can hear voices. It happens to ordinary people all over the world, all of the time. I'm certainly no genius, but twelve years ago when I was at a busy traffic junction intending to turn left, I distinctly heard a voice from nowhere telling me against all reason to turn right. If I had turned left there is no doubt in my mind that I would have been involved in a fatal collision involving two trucks and a car, a car that would have been mine.

Over the years many hundreds of people have written to me to tell me that they have heard or experienced similar unexplained warnings that saved them or their loved ones from danger. Stories like this incredible one sent to me by Elizabeth.

I saw an angel

When I was six – I'm fifty-six now – I saw an angel. It was early evening and I was sitting on a swing in the park behind our house. My brother had already gone home but I wanted to linger a while longer – in those days you had so much more freedom as a child. I decided to swing as high as I could. I worked my legs as hard as I could to go as high as I could. It felt like I was flying. It felt so real, in fact, that I did something really stupid. I jumped off the swing when it was really high thinking I could fly but I landed in a crumpled heap on the ground instead. Again, in those days, playgrounds didn't have softer ground to land on, just hard concrete. I felt a stab of pain through my left foot and I was bleeding from the palms of my hands where I had tried to break my fall. I tried to get up but it hurt too much, so I just sat there and howled. Nobody came. I started to get very frightened as it was getting darker and the shadows looked scary.

It was then that I saw an angel. She was floating about a foot or so from the ground and she was wearing a long-sleeved white dress that covered her feet and had sparkly bits down the front of it. She looked so tall, taller than any grown-up I had ever seen – at least seven foot. The thing I remember most is her face. It was white like her dress and she had a nose that looked like a button and white curly hair that floated over her back and shoulders. It was like a fan was blowing behind her. Best of all she brought light and the most enchanting musical sounds – it sounded a bit like a harp but there were so many instruments there and sounds I had never heard before. The dark shadows and the pain in my foot disappeared and I wasn't afraid of being alone any more. She held out a white hand towards me and I held onto it. It felt warm and strong as she gently led me in the direction of my house. I could hear her talking to me gently. I didn't understand what she was saying, but I knew they were words of comfort and love.

When I got home Mum immediately called a doctor. It turns out I had a broken ankle and the doctor said it was a miracle I was able to walk from the park to my house. I wanted to tell Mum what I had seen but I didn't think she would believe me so all these years I have never told anyone, except my twin sister who told me I imagined it. But I know what I saw and heard and know that what I experienced is very rare and lucky. It's such a relief to talk about it openly at last.

And following directly on with Tracey's story . . .

Always laughing

Last year my three-year-old daughter, Holly, started to talk to someone. When I asked her who she was talking to she said, 'My friends.' I'd read somewhere about children having imaginary friends so I didn't try to correct her or challenge her because they were real to her.

After a few months she started to talk to her friends every day. I could hear her talking to herself in her bedroom. Eventually, I decided to ask her what her friends looked like. She told me that she didn't know. Then I came into the kitchen one day and she was laughing as if she had heard a really funny joke. Another time when I was driving Holly looked out of the window, turned to me and asked me if she could put some of her toys into the sky. I didn't know what to think and asked her why, and she told me that her friends didn't have anything to play with. I asked her again what they looked like and she said, 'Big birds.' Now, birds have wings and so do angels. As far as I know she hasn't had any exposure to the idea of angels and as we aren't a religious family I haven't discussed such things with her either.

I don't know who she is talking to but what I do know is that they make her happy because she is always laughing. I finally decided to write to you because last night when I put her to bed and I was outside her bedroom folding some sheets I heard her say, 'Hi, Nana.' Nana is my grandmother and she died in 1980, twenty-nine years before Holly was born. My husband's mother died five years ago, so who was my daughter talking to?

I started with these two stories because they both involve the experiences of children. I would say that up to a third of the stories I receive every year concern children hearing or seeing angels. Research has shown that children definitely seem to have more psychic experiences than adults, and the main reason for that, in my opinion, is that children aren't worried about what other people might say or think. They haven't yet learned to question the truth or so-called reality of what they see. Trouble is, when we get older we worry so much about whether we have imagined things or not, that when our angels send us messages we are far more likely to dismiss or disbelieve them.

I always tell people who write to me asking why they don't seem to have psychic experiences that the first and most important step is to suspend disbelief and reconnect with the trusting child within. Your inner child is the piece of you that is spontaneous, trusting, innocent and joyful, and it is through your inner child that your angels will send their messages. Reconnecting with your inner child is easy to say but, as I know all too well, often hard to do. Perhaps damaging or painful experiences have made your inner child all but disappear. Perhaps the routines and demands of daily life have sapped your energy and enthusiasm or made you suspicious of things that can't be proved or don't seem logical. But whatever path your life has taken your inner child never completely fades away or loses its ability to understand the language that angels speak.

When I say the language that angels speak, I'm not talking about the New Testament's speaking in tongues. Perhaps many centuries ago the angels did communicate in this way, but this is no longer the case. Heaven is more likely to speak to you through loving thoughts and feelings that make immediate sense. On rare occasions, it can also speak – as was the case for Jenny in her story below – through a voice outside your head.

Give him to me

On December 6th last year I faced my worst fear. The day started normally enough with Sean, my five-month-old baby, screaming. I tried to settle him but he didn't seem to respond or want to feed, so I decided to give him some tough love and leave him alone for a bit while I showered and did some housework. I kept an eye on him while I tidied up and vacuumed and got a bit annoyed that the crying didn't ease. Also, he looked disorientated. Hard to explain when you're talking about a five month old, but it was like he was seeing things but wasn't seeing them. I put it down to the slight fever he had had the day before, or teething, and carried on with my chores.

About an hour later I felt triumphant because the sobbing seemed to have stopped. I picked Sean up and as I did I knew instantly that something was not right. Suspecting the worst, I checked his body all over for signs of a rash. When you're a new mum all the advertising and leaflets about meningitis are hard to ignore. I was mighty relieved when I found nothing.

For the next thirty or so minutes Sean continued to moan in my arms. He was making sounds I had never heard before and they began to scare me, so I decided to call my health visitor. She told me that it was probably nothing but if I was worried I should to take him to the doctor's surgery. I've always been a bit of a worrywart. When I was pregnant with Sean I was so scared of miscarrying I became a regular at my local surgery with some complaint or other. Eventually, my doctor told me that I might need to be referred to a counsellor for stress if I continued like this. I didn't want that on my medical records so I tried really hard to relax and stay calm. Also, I'd been to visit my doctor only a few days previously when Sean went down with a fever – going back so soon after that might be a mistake. I didn't want to be labelled a hysterical mum so I tried to soothe Sean as best I could. I cuddled and sang to him and put cold flannels on his head. None of it seemed to help so once again I decided to leave him alone in his cot for a bit in the hope he would drift off into a healing sleep.

I put Sean in his cot, drew the curtains and went to the kitchen to make a cup of tea. When the kettle started to whistle I heard this clear, calm voice tell me to take him to the doctor. I can't explain it very well. It sounded like my voice, but it was outside my head and it was so clear and calm I just knew I had to listen to it. I grabbed my car keys, wrapped Sean in a blanket and drove to the surgery.

When I got there I was told firmly by the receptionist that there were no free appointment times and it would be best if I called in for an appointment first thing in the morning. When I told her that my health visitor thought I should see a doctor today she reluctantly made me an appointment for after surgery, warning me that it would be quite a long wait. I told her that was fine.

I sat in the surgery and noticed that Sean was getting hotter and hotter in my arms. The screaming started again as well, and it was making me and everyone in the surgery tense. I walked him up and down trying to comfort him but nothing worked. Before long Sean was arching his back in my arms and was difficult to hold because he was so rigid. I went back to the receptionist and told her that I needed to see a doctor immediately. She told me to sit down and wait my turn.

I can't remember what I shouted next, but I'm sure it contained a few swear words. Just at that moment a doctor came into the receptionist's office, startled by all the commotion. He took one look at Sean and told me to come through to his office. Once inside, my heart stood still when he said the worst words I think I will ever hear, 'It could be meningitis.' I told him Sean had no marks on him and the doctor told me that in very rare cases this could happen.

What happened next is a bit of a blur. Sean was given a shot of something and then we were whisked away in an ambulance. I had been so stressed in the waiting room when the receptionist hadn't taken me seriously, but now they were taking me seriously I felt even worse. My throat throbbed with pain. When we got to the hospital Sean was given more injections and I was set up in a bed beside him. Exactly three hours later I was told that his situation had not improved and he needed to be moved to a specialist children's hospital.

An ambulance arrived to take him to the hospital. There wasn't enough room inside it for me because of the medics on board working on incubating him. They said it was best if I followed behind in a car. I felt sick as Sean's mouth was taped and a tube put in his throat. If I thought I was no stranger to panic and worry, I realised how wrong I was. Standing beside that ambulance I was frozen with panic – everything went into slow motion. Realising that it would be dangerous for me to drive, one of the medics grabbed someone and I was bundled into his car.

Driving to the new hospital was excruciatingly slow. I always thought that ambulances drove quickly but this one seemed to be going backwards. It felt like a funeral procession. At one point I lost sight of the ambulance. This was the first time Sean had ever been parted from

31

me. The pain of separation was unbearable and I felt that my head would burst. I wanted to scream, cry and rant but nothing came out of my mouth. I was frozen. Inside my head, though, I heard a thousand painful thoughts and the loudest was, 'It's your fault.' Perhaps if I had followed my intuition and taken Sean to a doctor sooner, none of this would have happened. With all my heart I begged for my son to be saved. Tears and mucus were streaming down my face. I offered my life in return for his.

It was at that moment, with the ambulance temporarily out of my sight, that I heard the clear, calm voice again. It was outside my head again and so loud I wondered how it was that the driver couldn't hear it. I held my breath.

'Jenny, he is already mine,' the voice said.

Wiping my eyes and my nose on my sleeve I looked all around me, convinced there was someone else in the car. Again the voice spoke to me. 'He is mine.'

At this point I thought I was losing it. Ever since Sean was born I had become increasingly compulsive and neurotic. It had started with me constantly tiptoeing into his room when he was sleeping to check he was breathing. Had I changed the batteries on the baby monitor? I rubbed my eyes hard to make sure this wasn't some foul nightmare. When I opened them I was sure I was awake. Once again the voice said, 'Jenny, he is mine.'

'He's not yours, he's mine, and you're not going to take him away,' I screamed out loud. My driver turned around briefly with a concerned look on his face. I asked him to drive faster. All that mattered right now was getting to Sean. If heaven was going to take his life back then I had to spend the last few moments with him. As these thoughts raced through my head, the word 'back' echoed loudly in my head. I realised then that Sean wasn't actually mine to keep or give away. His real home was heaven and he was just in my care while he was on earth.

I thought I had run out of tears, but even more flowed and in my heart I offered him back to heaven, to the place he had come from and to the place he truly belonged. If his life was meant to end today for reasons I could not understand, so be it.

This probably sounds astonishing to you – and it is still astonishing to me – but that moment when I was following my son in the ambulance was the most inspiring moment in my life. My heart was shattered but at the same time I wasn't scared any more, scared of what might happen. How could I lose what was not mine to keep? I understood deep down in my heart that he belonged to heaven.

By now the ambulance was back in sight and within minutes we had arrived at the hospital. Surprising myself with my calmness, I stepped out and followed the medical team as they rushed Sean into the hospital. I didn't complain when the nurses took me to the family room and told me it was best if I waited there. While I was there another mum brought me a cup of coffee and told me she understood. Her daughter was in a coma. It soon became clear to me that if anyone could understand, this woman could. Her child's life also hung in the balance.

I sat in that room for several hours and in the days that followed it became my home. I rarely went home to change my clothes. I didn't want to be away from Sean. My being a single mum, you would have thought it would be tough without the support of a partner, but my mother and my sister and the wonderful mums and dads in the family room gave me all the support I needed. One day when doctors told me to prepare for the worst I found myself, perhaps for the first time in my life, being the strong one. Mum and Annie – my sister – were in pieces, but somehow I kept it all together.

And then one morning I miraculously got the good news I had been longing for. Sean was going to be OK from now on. He had stabilised. There was still concern about long-term damage but he was going to live. The relief I felt was beyond words. I rushed into the family room and told the mum who had comforted me on my first day there my news. I was delirious with joy. She hugged me with such warmth, crying. She then told me that she had signed forms an hour before to turn her daughter's life support off. There was no sign of envy or bitterness in her, just joy for me and Sean.

I hugged her and ran to Sean. I stared at him just as I had stared at him the first time he was placed in my arms. I was afraid even to blink.

I learned so much from my experience, as terrible as it was. It has changed me in ways that I could never have imagined possible. When I needed it most the voice of an angel spoke to me and reminded me that we are all children of heaven. And when I needed it most I met people – like the mums and dads in that family room – who reminded me as never before of the standard of living in heaven.

Jenny's story is moving and astonishing and every time I read it – and I have read it many times – I get a lump in my throat. It also clearly shows some distinguishing characteristics that verify her experience as angelic. Unlike false guidance, which tends to be negative, critical, ego-centred and painful to hear, the messages Jenny heard were clear, direct, loving, urgent and positive.

Maria also believes that she heard the voice of an angel, but she heard it in a different way to Jenny. I think you will be intrigued by her story.

Taking it all in

I must have been twelve or thirteen, very young, when I first realised that my relationship with food wasn't the same as my friends'. I did wonder why I was so much heavier than girls my age. I started to put on masses of weight, and was always either thinking about food or eating. I was painfully shy and lacking in confidence, which made things worse. As a result, I started to eat more, as that was my only comfort and escape. I had my favourite foods – steak and kidney pudding being one of them – but sometimes I would eat vast amounts of any food I could grab, even if it didn't taste good to me. I had no idea how much I was eating. I was out of control, unable to stop.

By the age of nineteen, I weighed nearly twenty-one stone. I knew I had a problem but didn't think there was anyone who could help me. This was just the way I was. My form teacher did once urge me to see a doctor but I told him I had a slow metabolism. My family also ate huge amounts and were on the large side, like me, so not surprisingly they were not supportive. In my mind, feeling hungry all the time was just the way we were. When I was at school the taunts of other children who called me names and told me I was lazy and greedy also made me very suspicious and nervous around other people, especially boys.

I had a lot of emotional and family issues and the only way I knew to deal with my feelings was to eat and eat and eat. A week before my twenty-first birthday, I was a massive twenty-four stone. I was also chronically tired, hungry and depressed. I had no idea what to do. I didn't know of any way out. My family didn't care; I didn't have any friends. The only thing I could rely on was food. I knew I needed help, but there was no one.

The night before I turned twenty-one, my fridge broke. I came back from college and everything smelled sour. Even this didn't stop me and I ate everything inside it anyway, including a very dodgy tuna roll. Before long I was vomiting all over the kitchen floor. The stench was revolting. I fell into a heap on the kitchen floor and felt utterly worth-less and helpless. I couldn't move or get up. I couldn't even cry. I was alone in the universe. For some reason I started to talk out loud. I said I didn't believe in anything and I didn't care any more. I was tired and I was going to just sit there in my vomit. I was going to let the universe decide what to do with me.

As soon as I stopped talking I became aware of a faint voice – it was like a thought in my mind but not, if you know what I mean. It was my voice, but it wasn't. At first, I could hardly hear what it said because it was so faint, but I sat still and listened intently. It was telling me to be my own best friend.

Feeling lighter than I had for years, I got up feeling that there was an answer inside me, and that I was supported. In a nutshell, I felt hope. I grabbed a mop and cleaned up the kitchen floor. Then I emp-tied all the contents of my food cupboard into the bin. Then I ran a bath and sat in there for a good half an hour. I was doing what I thought a good friend would do for me, or advise me to do. I was stepping outside myself and taking care of me. I was becoming the best friend I had always longed for.

The next day, news of the terrible earthquake in Haiti hit the headlines. I'd never paid much attention to the news before but the terrible plight of all those people really hit me. They had lost everything and thousands and thousands were facing poverty and starvation. It felt like another sign. How could I keep feeling sorry for myself?

Over the next few days and months more lights went on in my life. I took it all in and began to realise that food was never going to satisfy my emotional and spiritual hunger. The only way to change my life was to change the way I felt about myself. I had to be the change I wanted to see in my life. If I wanted friends I had to become a friend to myself first.

Today, by following the loving guidance of my guardian angel's voice I have indeed become my own best friend. Working with my doctor, I'm eating healthily, and slowly but steadily losing the weight. I know I will get there in the end. This inner shift has caused a shift in how others treat me and I have even got a few real friends now. The lives of my family have also started to turn around and we are all losing weight together.

Maria's story differs from Jenny's in that Maria is convinced the voice came from inside rather than outside her head. It was a quiet inner voice that sounded like her own voice, but was somehow different, making her instantly recognise and accept it as the voice of spirit. I'm sure you will agree that this next brief story sent to me by Bethany is crystal-clear.

Driven to distraction

Last December I was driving along the motorway. As I usually am in the run-up to Christmas, I was fairly distracted and had a lot on my mind when I suddenly heard a voice – I don't know if it was male or female – call my name. It forced me to slow down and stop thinking about Christmas present lists and party ideas and concentrate on the road. Seconds later a plastic bag flew into my windscreen. I hit my brakes hard, just as a car ploughed into traffic meters ahead of me. I truly believe that if I had been driving faster and had remained as distracted as I was before I heard that voice call out to me, I would not be writing to you today.

Hearing your name called by a disembodied voice on waking, or when you are in a crowd or preoccupied with routine tasks like driving, as was the case for Bethany in her story above, is a frequently reported way for spiritual beings to speak to you. It's possible that it is easier for spirits to greet us when we are distracted by others, or just waking up in the morning, because our minds are more open to psychic communication when we are relaxed.

And sometimes you may not hear your name being called, but experience it in another way, as Fiona's interesting story shows.

Outgoing message

Our mother passed away on 19 January 1996. So every year I would travel down to stay overnight with my sister, Anna, on 18 January so we could spend Mum's anniversary together. We wouldn't get all morbid or anything. Usually, we just sat and chatted – typically about Mum – but it was just that we were always close, and because we were together when Mum passed, we felt we should honour her anniversary together too.

Sadly, and devastatingly, my sister passed away on 29 October 2006. She was only forty-three – and my only comfort was, and still is, that she and Mum are together. and free from the illnesses that claimed them.

Anyway, shortly after Anna passed away, my son started a new job, which meant he was working through the nights, coming home early in the mornings and going straight to bed. On 18 January 2007, I was out shopping, and I got a text message, apparently from my son, which simply read 'Fiona'. Of course, I thought this was strange – he never would address me by my name – so I tried calling him. No answer. So as soon as I got home, I went up to his room. He was sound asleep, and his mobile, which would normally be right by his bed (he used it as his alarm), was out in the middle of the floor! And when I checked it – there were no outgoing messages!

I believe that somehow, Anna had managed to contact me on the first anniversary of Mum's passing since she herself passed – and the first anniversary we wouldn't actually be together. I talk to the angels all the time. Every night I thank them for the blessings in my life – and ask them to pass on my love to all my loved ones in heaven.

As Fiona's story shows, angels are not against using modern technology to communicate with us. Many of the stories sent to me feature mobiles, iPods, computers and the like, showing how angels can adapt themselves to the era they are in.

There can often be a reason – a warning, typically – why angels call your name, but more often than not it is simply a form of friendly greeting from beyond the grave. But it's not just your name that angels can call out. Sometimes, as in Samantha's story below, they will use other words or thoughts to get your attention.

Falling back

One day I was driving behind some people who had furniture on the back of their Ute. In my head something or someone told me to change lanes just in case something fell off the back. I changed lanes and, as soon as I had, a drawer from a table fell off the back of the Ute, smashing on the road. Was this my mind saying to move over or was it something else? I believe it was something else.

Jackie is in no doubt that she heard reassuring words from beyond.

Tale of two rings

I am eighteen years old. After reading your book I had a strong urge to email you. I have had a few experiences with angels myself. There is one experience that sticks in my mind and I replay it almost every day.

When I was seven my family moved from England to Wales, and I soon thought I knew my way around my village pretty well. However, when I was thirteen, I was walking back from a friend's house. She had recently moved and I suddenly became disorientated. I took a wrong turning and was scared to move anywhere. As I was about to turn around, I saw a shadow of a figure standing behind me. I put my arms out and turned around in a full circle and realised nothing was there. Then I heard a man's voice that sounded familiar to me, and it told me to walk forward and trust him and listen to his voice and instructions. With the voice I smelled an old aftershave that I remember smelling when I was a child.

I trusted the voice and followed his instructions, and while I was walking the figure told me that he was proud of me and how I had turned out as a person. He also told me that my great-grandmother (big Nan) was proud of me too and couldn't have asked for a greater great-granddaughter. I followed the voice and after half an hour I found myself outside my house. Before I walked inside, the voice told me to look in my jewellery box, and that there I would find two rings — one was his and the other was my big Nan's. I went to my box and found the two rings, and later found out that they had belonged to my great-granddad.

It is rare to hear the voice of an angel at the end of the telephone line, but that is exactly what happened to Camilla, as she explains.

The secret

When I was about nine, my grandma was still alive. The last few years of her life must have been terrible for her as she suffered from Alzheimer's. I remember when my parents took me to see her in the nursing home and she just seemed to be wasting away. I was really scared to see someone so frail but my parents wanted me to visit her before she died.

A week after this I was sitting in the kitchen doing my homework when Mum's mobile phone rang. I called Mum to answer it but she was busy upstairs and asked me to. I rummaged through her bag and took the call. It was Grandma.

'Hello. It's Grandma here. Don't worry. Everything will be all right. Tell your parents. Don't worry. Everything's going to be fine.'

So I hung up and told my mum what Grandma had said but she didn't believe me because Grandma was too ill to be using phones. An hour later we received a call from my great-aunt. She told us that my grandma had died about an hour ago. This freaked me out as this was exactly the time I had received my phone call.

I didn't remind my mum about the phone call as I knew she still wouldn't believe me. It's a secret that I've kept with me all this time and it is wonderful to be able to finally share it now with other believers.

Both Camilla and Jackie believe they actually heard the voice of an angel – and you'll find plenty more amazing stories like this later in the book – but it is important to point out here that such strikingly overt communications or encounters are rare. All the people in this next batch of stories heard their angels speak in gentler, subtler ways. They may not be as dramatic, but the impact on their lives certainly was. None of the people here actually heard angel voices, but all the same they remained convinced that their angels sent them powerful, life-changing communications. I'm going to begin with Michael's uplifting story:

Flying high

I'm a travel writer and I'm often sent on assignments abroad. About two years ago I was on a plane feeling depressed and lonely. I loved my job but the long hours and roaming lifestyle make long-term relationships impossible. The longest I've ever been with someone was a year and as I was flying home that day, I was once again flying home to an empty flat. It wasn't just the loneliness, I was also going through a kind of midlife crisis because in a month's time I was hitting the big four-oh, and I had very little to show for it. No family, no house and not much in the bank, considering the hours I put into my work. This wasn't the first time I had felt low. In the previous five years returning home had always triggered this kind of reflection. Mercifully, I never had to deal with it too long because after a few days back home I'd be posted on another assignment far away.

So there I was feeling sorry for myself. Sleep seemed the best option, so I put my blinkers on and tried to settle down. I couldn't, though, because there were two women sitting beside me (I was in a row of three), both with headphones on and engrossed in a movie, and they kept laughing really loud. Eventually, the movie finished and they spent several minutes regurgitating the plot. Then, when I thought it might all be over and they would settle down, they started talking about someone they knew called Hero who had just been diagnosed with colon cancer.

I heard them say that this woman had just started to get her life together after her husband walked out on her, leaving her to raise two children alone. They said how terrifying it must be as a mother to know that she might not survive to see her children become adults. Instead

43

of crumbling with fear, though, this woman had started her own business and a university degree. She had told her friends that if she was going to die, she was going to die living life to the full.

Even though I didn't know this woman, the warm way that her friends talked about her made me feel as if I did know her, and her name seemed to describe her personality perfectly. Since then I've often thought of this brave lady appropriately named Hero. If I am flying home from an assignment and feeling sorry for myself, I imagine her living every moment of her life to the full, as she promised her friends she would. When depression tries to silence happiness and warmth and I regret the decisions I have made in my life, I think of her. If she could pursue her dreams despite the threat of actual cancer, then surely I could find direction and hope in my life, despite my cancer of the soul.

I used to think that a mentor was someone who knew you really well and who could guide and inspire you for months and years. But I have never met my mentor. Just happening to overhear a conversation about her was enough for me to inhale a bit of her spirit. I've never met my Hero, but I believe in her. Is it perhaps the same with angels? Even if you don't think you have encountered one, believing in them can be life-transforming.

I wrote back to tell Michael that it was no coincidence he sat next to those ladies that day. His guardian angel guided him to that seat. Overhearing a conversation in which a stranger says just the thing you need to hear at exactly the right time in your life can be an incredible experience. It's happened to me several times in my life, and each time it has happened it has filled me with a sense of awe. One memory stands out in particular. It happened twenty-five years ago when I was trying to get a job in publishing and failing miserably. I was sitting on a bench at a train station waiting for my train when a couple of guys sat next to me and started discussing a job interview one of them had in the morning, for a 'new age' imprint of books at a certain publishing house. I heard the guy saying that he needed to do some reading-up that night because he didn't know anything about 'spirits and stuff' – but I did. The next morning I applied for the job and got it.

I'm convinced my angels wanted me to overhear that conversation because it was yet another stepping stone to my angel writing career, and ever since, I have always paid attention to conversations I happen to overhear. I'm not suggesting here that you eavesdrop on conversations you are not a part of. That would be wrong, as angel messages are only sent in natural and unthreatening ways. What I am suggesting is that if you do find yourself in a position where you can overhear naturally, for example in a restaurant, plane or train, you may just want to listen carefully. You never know what messages heaven might be sending your way.

In much the same way, many people have written to me to tell me that they have found themselves inexplicably drawn towards buying a newspaper or magazine they would not ordinarily buy and then when they read that newspaper or magazine there is a story or report relevant to them. Another common experience is when you are in a bookshop or a library perhaps unconsciously looking for guidance and suddenly a book will fly off a shelf and drop at your feet. Many people have written to me to tell me that this is how they stumbled across one of my books or another book that helped give them a fresh perspective. This is angels at work – trust in them and you will hear their message.

Melanie, whose story is below, believes her angels guide her towards messages contained in books.

Points of light

I see myself as a survivor of a traumatic life, including extreme abuse and major losses. It is difficult to describe such prolonged emotional suffering but from about the age of five I have been comforted by my awareness of and belief in an unseen world. I have always felt close to heaven and the angels. I have many stories to relate but for now I want to tell you about one as an example of many others.

Back in the 1990s my adoptive mother was taken in a car accident. We had had a volatile relationship and been estranged for several years, but our relationship remained unresolved and her death shocked me severely. Various things happened after her funeral and they have convinced me that she is watching over me. For example, I began to hear her whispering my name. I was afraid at first but then I replied in my head and the whispering stopped. One night I woke up and my bedroom was illuminated with golden light. One outstanding event: I was in town crying about her death when I suddenly felt this powerful and unexplained 'urge' to visit the charity shop. I entered and felt guided towards a shelf full of dull paperback books. Without looking I pulled one out and the title read: *Points of light: A mother's love is eternal.*

The cover was illustrated with a starry sky (I love astronomy) and a mother close to her two small children. Part of the novel repeats my experience of hearing whispers and other unusual occurrences. I was totally astonished and treasure the book still. I believe I was meant to buy that book.

One possibly unexpected place to find angels speaking to us is in numbers or number sequences on clocks, watches, phone numbers, on license plates or buildings, and so on. The number 11, and multiples of it such as 22, 44 and 55, is especially associated with the presence of angels watching over you and trying to open your mind to their loving guidance and protection. One of the most commonly reported experiences I have discovered in recent years is glancing at a clock and it reading 11.11. It's not just the number 11, of course, that has special significance and meaning. Every number and number combination can resonate with meaning, and part of the joy of discovering numbers is to search for their meaning. Numerology is an age-old science and one I would love to delve deeper into here if I had the word count, but sadly I don't. All I can do is encourage you to learn more so when you start noticing number patterns in your life, you can unravel the meanings and hidden messages from your angels yourself.

The word 'angel' is another common way for the angels to let us know they are with us. Sometimes if you ask for angelic help, you will hear the word 'angel' mentioned in a song on the radio or on television, or you will read it online or in a book or magazine or someone will say the word to you in the most unlikely context.

And don't forget that you can hear heavenly voices simply through reading angel stories, like the ones you are reading right now in this book. You can read it at just the right time when you need comfort, guidance or inspiration or are not sure what to do next. It can speak to you. It can open your mind. It can open your heart – the place where angels live. And it's not just words, numbers and books that your angels can speak to you with. If you hear a song repeatedly in your head or on the radio, it could just be heaven-sent, as it was for Joanne.

My grandma moment

My grandma passed away three years ago now after battling multiple myeloma. She was like my second mum and I still miss her terribly. In the car on the way to the funeral everyone around me was talking, but I was so devastated I couldn't speak, I was just staring out of the windows, tears streaming down my face – I have never known grief like it. In my head I was thinking, 'I love you, Grandma, why did you have to go and leave us?' then suddenly the song 'You Raise Me Up' started playing in my head over and over. It's not a song that specifically meant anything between me and my grandma, but somehow the words gave me comfort.

For weeks after the funeral I couldn't stop crying. I was driving in my car one day, tears in my eyes, having what I called 'a grandma moment'. I put the radio on, to try and give me something else to think about so I could concentrate on driving, and the next song played was 'You Raise Me Up'. Again it gave me comfort, and made me wonder if perhaps she hasn't left me, but is still around watching over me. It may be coincidence but I like to believe that she is.

Music is a beautiful way for angels to speak to us, as you'll see in Terry's account below.

Peace came over me

I have just finished reading your book *An Angel Healed Me*, and it has prompted me to write to you regarding an experience I had quite some time ago now. When in my teens, I thought I could swim, so with my mates I ventured down to the River Severn, which is nearby. Having dived in I quickly discovered to my dismay that my legs were like lead and I was trying to swim in an upright position (impossible), taking on board lots of water through shouting for help and panicking. Fortunately, my friend swimming nearby saw what was happening and managed to pull me to safety.

What I experienced during that episode, when I was actually drowning, was this: a sort of peace came over me and I heard the most wonderful music, just like a big choir singing all around me. Nobody around me heard a thing when I questioned them later. Was my guardian angel at my side helping my friend rescue me?

Some years later when at a friend's funeral, I was standing at his graveside looking down on his coffin and again I heard the most wonderful music, exactly the same as I had previously heard, coming up from the grave! Nobody else heard anything. Was I privileged once again?

Divine communications can also manifest in your dreams, as they clearly did for Fiona and her sister.

Ending in a hug

Since Mum passed I have had different experiences, most often a sense of her being near me with her distinctive sense of humour! I think the most wonderful experience, though, was when my sister and I had the same dream about Mum, on the same night. Slight differences – but basically, we were both with her, talking with her, and our visits ended in a hug. We lived over a hundred miles apart, so I called her the following day to tell her about my dream, and she told me about hers – and we both commented, 'Didn't that hug feel wonderful!'

Hazel sent this remarkable dream story my way.

The key

When I was a young mum in my late twenties I lived with my family at one end of a very long road. At the other end of the road lived another young mum – I'll call her Alison. I didn't have much to do with her, only on occasion I saw her at the local school that our children attended. Anyway, one night I dreamt of Alison, in fact in the dream I was her and I was so depressed, unhappy, sad – oh it was a terrible dream. I woke up and thought, I hope that was just a dream and not how she really feels.

Later that morning after the usual rush to get three little ones off to school I heard a knock on my door. Amazingly there on my doorstep was Alison (she had never visited me before). 'Could you look after the key for me?' she said, 'And give it to my children when they come home from school? I have left a note on the door to tell them where to come.'

'Of course I will,' I said, then (because of the dream!), 'but first come in for a few minutes before you go out, and have a coffee.' She came in, protesting she didn't really have time, but I was insistent. 'Alison, are you all right?' I said. 'Please tell me if something is wrong.' With that she burst into tears and confessed she had found out her husband was having an affair, she had taken an overdose, and she was getting out of the house to die!!! I dialled 999, got an ambulance and she went to hospital and had her stomach pumped.

Dreams are such a potent and powerful way for angels to speak to us that I will return to them in more detail later in the book. For now just bear in mind that angels love to communicate with you in many ways, and because dreams are a gentle, understated way for them to make contact, they may well choose to manifest to you first through this medium.

Sadly, many of us don't pay enough attention to messages from the other side that come to us in our dreams and that is why our angels may sometimes choose more direct methods, for example phones or doorbells that ring but when they are answered no one is there. Despite this, the person is left with a powerful sense that a departed loved one is trying to get in touch. John's story is a fine example of this phenomenon:

Unexpected

My wife died a week before our thirtieth wedding anniversary. She had a heart attack. It was all very sudden and unexpected and my only consolation was that the doctors told me she would not have suffered, or even known what was going on. I had hardly any memories of adult life without her. She was the most wonderful woman. I could write a book about her. One of her most endearing qualities was that you could never second-guess her. She had such a youthful spirit and was always urging me to seek adventure and magic in life. She was beautiful on the inside and the outside. Sure, we had our tough times, as any married couple has, but we worked through them and our relationship was the stronger for it.

Our being so close, you can imagine how black my life felt when I spent my first night without her, but I don't think I was alone and, after reading one of your books, I just had to send you my story. It must have been about two in the morning when I heard a ringing sound. Numb with grief, I just tried to blank it out but the ringing was persistent. It rang twenty or so times then stopped for a few minutes, then started up again.

The ringing got louder and louder and it dawned on me that it was coming from my room. I got up and eventually tracked it down to under my bed. I'm not as agile as I used to be so it took a while to crouch down and look underneath and when I did I saw a smallish parcel wrapped in red ribbon. I picked it up and sat on my bed and saw that it was a gift to me from my wife. She must have bought it for my approaching fiftieth birthday. I tore it open and it was a mobile phone. I wasn't interested in that; I was only interested in the card my wife had handwritten. In it she told me that she loved me for ever and it was time for me to stop being so old-fashioned and to have my own mobile phone. My reluctance to use computers or own a mobile phone had been a source of constant discussion between me and my wife. She loved the technology. I hated it.

I grabbed the phone and held it to my heart and eventually drifted off into an uneasy sleep. The next morning I told my son he could have the phone because the card was all I really wanted. Hearing it ringing the whole night before was enough for me. My son took the phone and told me it couldn't have been ringing because it hadn't even been charged yet. While he was speaking I had a ringing sensation in my ears. When the ringing stopped I looked at my son and in that instant – don't tell me how – we both knew that this was my wife's way of reaching out to us from the other side, letting us know that even though we couldn't see or touch her any more she was still very much with us.

Hardly a day goes by when I don't draw comfort from that phone ringing. It rings quite a lot these days as I took my wife's advice and learned how to use it. Each time I answer it or use it I feel indescribably close to my wife. I'm aware this may not make sense to a lot of people, but it makes perfect sense to me, because she always told me to expect the unexpected.

In his story John mentions the sensation of ringing in the ears. If you aren't sure what I am talking about here, I don't mean the harsh and painful grating noise associated with medical conditions, such as tinnitus, but a gentle, high-pitched ringing sound that only lasts for a few moments then fades away. Several mediums have told me that they believe this ringing sound is a sign that heaven is trying to communicate with you, sending guidance and reassurance into your unconscious where it will manifest in vivid dreams and flashes of intuition. I always feel warm and loved when I hear this gentle ringing and many people have written to me to say that it has a similar calming influence on them.

And sometimes angels will speak to us in response to questions we ask – not just ones that are spoken out loud but also ones that come from our hearts. A few years ago my husband and I were having problems managing our work schedules and regrettably the kids had to spend a lot of time during the week with babysitters, when they weren't at school. I had to work because we needed the money, but I worried all the time that I wasn't giving my kids the love and support and time they needed.

I struggled on as best I could until one day it all got too much. I was trying to get supper on but feeling stressed and tired. The kids were cranky and fighting over which programme to watch on TV. Out loud I said, 'How can I make this work?' As soon as I said it there was a power cut. After the initial panic, the silence and peace was blissful. I got some candles out and we all sat down together.

The power cut lasted about forty-five minutes, but it felt like five minutes as we chatted and giggled. Free from distractions, and most of all free of the TV blaring, it was wonderful. I was almost disappointed when the power came back and realised there and then that my angels had answered me. Simply turning off the TV and spending time talking about things was exactly what we all needed.

Danusia, who shares her amazing story below, also found that an answer came in response to questions she was asking herself. I know you are going to like her story. I haven't yet found a person that didn't.

Lucky numbers

I would like to tell you my story. The whole of my life I have had feelings of déjà vu, or intuition, where things happen and I feel I already knew they would happen, but four years ago something happened that can only be described as extraordinary. In August 2006 I was in financial dire straits. I had been there before and lost everything including my home, and couldn't believe I had got to that position again, especially as I had worked so hard in getting myself and my children back on our feet. I was just about ready to give up the fight and feeling quite sorry for myself and angry with myself as I sat in my bedroom surrounded by my bills and debts, filling out a form to put my finances into the hands of a debt agency, so as not to lose my home again! It was 5 August 2006, I had the TV on in the background and the National Lottery was about to start.

I said out loud, 'Can anyone help me? If there's anyone up there who can help me, now would be a really good time!' and promised to be better with money in the future. I wasn't taking much notice of the TV as I was concentrating on filling out this agency form, but as the first of the draws started taking place I could hear some familiar numbers being called out. I looked up at the TV screen and instantly recognised some of the numbers being drawn as mine, so naturally thought I'd probably won ten pounds. Quickly, I decided to write the draw numbers down on the envelope of one of my bills to look at later.

I went back to filling out the form but my eyes kept being drawn back to this envelope with the Thunderball Lottery numbers on it, and I decided to get my ticket out of my handbag and check my ten-pound win for sure. But to my amazement my ticket numbers matched all six of the numbers on the envelope. I thought how stupid I was to have written my own numbers on the back of the envelope, and did not think for one minute that I could actually have won the jackpot. I had to then wait until the end of the lottery show when they put all the draw numbers on the screen again for confirmation. I could not believe my eyes when they did because I checked, rechecked and checked again: I had indeed got all six numbers. I had won the jackpot of £250,000.

This was unbelievable, and I could only put it down to my plea earlier for help, that someone was truly watching over me and had answered my prayers, but to answer so quickly was indeed a miracle! (If you google my name – Danusia Phillips – you will see newspaper reports, etc. of my win.)

I often used to be reluctant to ask my angels for practical help, especially money, feeling as if material concerns contaminated spiritual ones, but increasingly over the years I have learned that the angels do sometimes answer our prayers for practical help. However, before you rush off to beg your angels to give you next week's lottery numbers, may I sound a note of caution.

Although the angels may sometimes guide us to unexpected sources of money when times are tough, it doesn't always work like that and I don't want you to get the wrong idea. Your guardian angel is unlikely to give you the lottery numbers because in the world of spirit money or wealth really has no meaning. Angels aren't interested in money because they know that money does not bring happiness and means nothing in the world of spirit, unless you put your money to good use. For proof of that you need only read celebrity magazines or the newspapers to see how confused, unhappy and needy many of the rich and famous people in the world are. The purpose of angels is to offer love and healing. It is the richness of your soul they are interested in, not your bank balance.

The purpose of this chapter was simply to give you an introductory snapshot of some of the many ways angels can manifest themselves in our lives today. I'll be returning to many of the themes raised here in more detail later in the book, but I hope you are beginning to see that angels can speak in many different voices. If you keep your mind and your heart open, there is no right or wrong way to hear your guardian angel.

Perhaps you may be wondering at this stage in the book if spiritual beings have already spoken to you in your life, as they did for the people whose stories you've read in this chapter, but you didn't recognise them for what they were at the time. The very fact that you are wondering suggests to me that your angels have already been calling out to you, and they could even be calling out to you right now as you read this book.

This was quite literally the case for Kim.

Baby Liam

I don't know why I'm writing this at nearly one in the morning! But I can't help it! I feel compelled to do so! And that is very unlike me.

This afternoon I was shopping with my friend and my daughter when I saw something that made me stop dead in my tracks. It was your angel book. Well, I went straight in and bought it. I just had to have it. You see, the young child on the cover is the spitting image of my daughter! I couldn't believe it! Same eyes, same mouth, hair, everything!

At about midnight tonight, I was lying in bed and I just couldn't fall asleep. I just had to get up and get this book. My fifteen-month-old daughter Chloe was sound asleep in her room and I could hear her snoring. Once I got the book and settled myself back in bed, I opened the first page. Before I could even start to read I heard Chloe start to babble. I didn't pay too much attention at first as she has been babbling a lot recently but then she said something that made me run to her!

'Babble, babble, babble. Baby Liam. Liam, baby, baby, baby Liam, Liam,' and then laughter. I went into her room and she was sitting pointing to the top of her wardrobe at a box and repeated herself a few more times. She then lay down again and went straight to sleep. Before I could even turn around to leave the room she was snoring again.

There is no way she could ever have known about Liam.

Three years ago on 14 July 2007 I lost a little boy and called him Liam. Now nearly three years to the anniversary of his death, here was my fifteen-month-old daughter, who could only say the usual gibberish most children her age can say, calling out his name. I have never told her about her brother, not yet anyway. Also, the box she was pointing to on top of the wardrobe is the box with all his things in that I kept, some clothes, toys and so on. There are a number of boxes on that wardrobe but she was pointing to his.

I have recently been working with a charity called Angel Babies that helps families that have lost children. Is this all a sign he's here? I can't shake these goosebumps off! I feel like he's here and my daughter knows it too!

When I went back to my bed the page I had marked before running into Chloe's bedroom was the page with your contact details. Nothing like this happens to me, and I haven't even read the first page of your book yet!! I can already tell I won't be able to put it down!

I wrote back to tell Kim that I was convinced her little Liam was reaching out to her, reassuring her that his life hadn't ended and he was very much alive on the other side. The loving bond between mother and child is so intense and so strong it cannot be broken by death.

Your birthright

Although earlier in this chapter I mentioned children as particularly receptive to divine messages, and Kim's wonderful story above closes this chapter once again with a story about a child, I want to make it clear here that everyone whatever their age or background has the ability to hear angels speak to them because everyone, and I stress everyone, is born with psychic powers. It is your birthright, your gift from heaven. Some people may appear to be more psychic or spiritual than others, but this is only because these people are willing to open their minds and their hearts with the loving trust of a child. In other words, if you stop worrying about whether you are psychic or not, barriers of fear and doubt are removed and it is so much easier for your angels to speak to you.

If you don't think heaven is talking to you, it could be that a message has been sent but you've not recognised it, or perhaps you aren't ready to hear the answer. My advice is to keep on asking your angels to reveal themselves and with persistence and patience it will happen eventually. There have been many times in my life when I felt my angels weren't answering my questions. Sometimes I felt completely abandoned by them but deep down I never really stopped hoping for their guidance and insight. Lack of self-confidence, doubt and fear may have blocked me from picking up on them for many years, but in time I did finally connect with them and hear celestial voices in my own way.

So, if you take anything away with you from this book I hope it will be that you understand, really understand, that you don't need to be a child or a medium or a psychic to hear your angels. Heaven is speaking to you all the time, offering you protection, comfort and guidance – you just haven't been listening or noticing the messages flying in your direction, because they often appear in ways you least expect them to.

In the next few chapters I've gathered together more astonishing true stories in the hope that they will inspire you further to find your own special ways to recognise, understand and truly hear your own angel voices.

CHAPTER 3

The Language of Angels

And now here is my secret, a very simple secret: It
is only with the heart that one can see rightly; what
is essential is invisible to the eye.

Antoine de Saint-Exupéry

In the previous chapter you saw that angels don't always use spoken or written words to convey their messages – sometimes they can communicate through a kind of telepathy, filling your mind with thoughts that you know to be true and meaningful. In this chapter I'm going to delve deeper into this very common but frequently neglected form of angel communication.

Has this ever happened to you? You don't know why, because you may not have the evidence to support it, but deep down inside you just know that you are correct, or that you are on to something or can clearly see the bigger picture and your hunch turns out to be correct. Many people will call this intuition, sixth sense or gut instinct, but whatever you call it I believe that angels can communicate with us through divinely inspired thoughts, ideas and revelations, and such inspiration and insight is, along with love itself, the language that angels speak.

We all have intuition, that still, quiet and knowing voice within us. Intuition tells us when we are on the right track. It is an insight that seems to come out of nowhere, a sudden knowledge without any logical evidence. It is truth without reason. If we develop it deeply enough we can find it the most useful guiding tool we could possibly wish for. In Latin the word intuition means 'in to you', and theologian Florence Scovel Shinn once said, 'Intuition is a spiritual faculty that doesn't explain, but simply points the way.' In other words, it is your guardian angel talking to you.

This doesn't mean that your angels impress things on your mind, because they cannot use what isn't in your realm of experience, but it does mean that they can focus your mind on what really matters.

If you would stop for a moment and ponder this concept, you would begin to realise the incredible power there already is inside you – that every answer to every question is already right there within you. And you don't even have to get any special training to start using it. All you need to do is open your mind, trust in the miraculous and ask your angels to guide you. Remember that it is music to the angels' ears to hear your requests for assistance because each request is an acknowledgement of their presence.

All the people whose stories are in this chapter believe that angels spoke to them through an inner voice, and when they listened to what heaven was trying to say to them the impact on their lives was life-changing. When I first read this story sent to me by Juliet a few months ago, I just knew it had to have a prominent place in this chapter, so here it is.

Putting my foot down

This happened to me six months ago in a supermarket car park and each time I think of it shivers run down my spine. If I hadn't trusted my intuition my life would have changed for ever.

It was raining, pelting down, and I wanted to be in and out of the supermarket to do my weekly shop as quickly as possible. I did my shop and struggled through the wind and rain back to my car with my trolley. There were no cars parked beside or in front of me so I placed my trolley alongside the boot of my car, loaded everything in and returned the trolley to the store. Then I jumped into my car, started up the engine and released the handbrake. I was keen to get home in the warm and put the kettle on but something stopped me putting my foot on the accelerator.

It was as if my mind would not let me move my foot. It was crazy really because I was tired, cold, wet and hungry and I wanted to get home fast, but I wouldn't let me. The best way I can think of describing it is like when your eyes get stuck on one spot and you find it hard to move them away. That's how it felt with my foot – it wasn't listening to my brain. I looked in my rear-view and side mirrors and there was nothing. I turned my head around and there was nothing, but still my foot wouldn't do what I was telling it to do.

It was beyond crazy. Was I just going to sit there? I sure wasn't, so I bent down, grabbed my foot with both hands and placed it on the pedal. Once again I looked in the rear-view mirror but this time I saw the tip of a little girl's head moving from side to side. I got out of my car and saw that she must have been about three years old and she was splashing about in a puddle directly behind my car. Her mother was a few parking spaces away from me strapping her other children into the car.

Bored of waiting, the little girl must have run from puddle to puddle until she found the largest and most satisfying puddle to splash in directly behind my car. Both mother and child had no idea of the potential danger of the situation. When I had got in my car my mind had been focused on only one thing – getting home quickly – and if had done as I intended that child would have died, that mother's life would have been torn apart and, even though it would not have been my fault because there is no way I could have seen such a small child in my rear-view and side mirrors, I would have found it very difficult to live with myself after such a tragedy.

I truly believe that my guardian angel and that little girl's guardian angel joined forces that day and stopped me putting my foot down. I can't tell you how happy and relieved I am that I listened to my intuition, or as you say in your angel books my guardian angel, that rainy day.

Evie is equally glad she listened to her intuition.

Big bang

I had just got home from a trip to the park with my four-year-old son. I asked him if he needed to go to the bathroom and he said yes so I took him. Then we went into the kitchen to make some toast and hot chocolate. While I was getting the bread out and gently warming the milk in a pan, I got the strangest sensation. It was as if cold chills were running down my spine. Even though we had just been out I felt that we should go out again. It didn't feel right being at home so I turned off the stove, picked my son up, grabbed our coats and my purse and headed out the door. I was seconds away from closing the front door when everything went into slow motion. I heard a big bang come from inside the house and found myself falling over with my son in my arms. We suffered a few cuts and bruises, and my son was terrified, but the important thing was that we were both OK.

There had been a gas explosion in our house – apparently gas had been leaking silently into the house for several days and I hadn't noticed. Putting the stove on to warm the milk was probably the trigger.

Do you think it was my guardian angel or my intuition that saved me and my son that day? If I hadn't followed my instincts and left, there is every possibility I would not be writing this letter to you today.

I wrote back to tell Evie that her guardian angel and her intuition are one and the same. Many people make the mistake of thinking they are somehow separate, but they are both manifestations of the divine forces that exist within and all around us.

Tayler sent me this email:

The button

I always used to think that guardian angels were winged beings with halos. I had heard stories about people who believed they had seen angels and although I wanted to believe in them I couldn't. I've changed my mind though after something extraordinary happened to me last year.

I was tidying up the front room after putting my daughter down to sleep in her cot when I got this urge to go back and check on her, even though there were no sounds of distress or crying coming from the monitor. I went back to her bedroom and peeped through the door. I didn't get close because I didn't want her to see me. She was moving about but there was no crying and she seemed absolutely fine so I went back to my chores.

When I got back to the living room it felt as if I couldn't breathe. I started to cough and splutter and as I did the urge to check on my daughter again was overwhelming. I ran back to her room and went right over to her cot. I picked her up and could see she was struggling to breathe. I opened her mouth and saw a button stuck in her throat. It must have come from the soft toy her nana had knitted for her which had two buttons for eyes. I cursed my stupidity for letting her sleep with it in the cot. I managed to dislodge the button with my little finger and I have never been so pleased to hear my daughter cry. The button must have been slowly cutting off her air supply.

Tayler also told me that she will never again doubt her hunches and feelings, especially when they concern her children and don't seem to make sense at the time. Gary, whose story is below, feels the same way.

Missing out

I'm a fitness manager at a well-known chain of gyms. When someone new joins the gym my job is to design them a fitness programme, or get one of my instructors to, and if they are committed they can follow it and it will help them improve their health and fitness, or lose weight if need be.

I get dozens of new sign-ups each week and hundreds of people who need follow-up programmes designed when they find their current ones have got too easy, so I have a lot on my plate. No surprise, a lot of the people that sign up to the gym don't take up their fitness programme, or if it is designed for them follow it through. It's not my job to chase them up but for some reason I can't explain I got this sign-up and I noticed that there had been no follow-up with the fitness programme. It was for a woman in her late fifties, a non-smoker and mother of five.

Over the next few days this woman – whom I had never met before – kept popping up in my mind. There were plenty more non-sign-ups but her non-response kept worrying me. I decided to email. There was no response so I left a message on her mobile, asking her to contact the gym. Again there was no response so I left another message. Two days later this lady came in and asked me to design a fitness programme for her. It gave me great satisfaction because her blood pressure was fairly high and exercise was going to be of great benefit. She stuck with that fitness programme and even introduced her sister to the gym.

A while later, her sister confided in me that joining this gym was the best thing that could have happened to her family. Apparently, after joining the gym this lady – I don't want to give her name – had found out that her husband was having an affair and was leaving her after twenty years of marriage and five kids. She was extremely depressed and even thought of ending it all, but my contacting her from the gym had shown her that there was life outside marriage and a way forward.

Going to the gym got her out of the house and gave her a goal, some-thing to work towards. I still can't believe it while I am writing to you, but I do think my intuition saved that lady's life, or at the very least gave her something to move forward with.

I couldn't agree with Gary more. I am convinced that his intu-ition may well have saved that lady's life. Something similar happened to me about eight years ago. It isn't as dramatic a story as Gary's, in that following my intuition didn't save another person's life, but it may just have helped transform it.

As soon as my son learned to walk, like many new mums, I was keen to take him to mother and toddler groups to help him socialise and for me to compare notes with other mums. On one occasion I signed up for a music and movement class, but when I got there I found it hard to concentrate on the activities because my thoughts were drawn to a rather quiet woman sitting oppo-site me with her daughter. Unlike the other mums she didn't seem as bright-eyed and excited when she introduced herself and her daughter Charlotte to the group. It was clear that she loved Charlotte because there was no shortage of kisses and cuddles, but something wasn't right.

It really got to me so at the end of the class, I decided to intro-duce myself. She was very pleasant but I could see that she was also close to tears. To ease the situation I tried to make her smile by introducing my son to her daughter. My son tried to say her daugh-ter's name but it came out as Charlie. Then he grabbed her hands and said, 'Charlie, bye-bye.' This seemed to be too much for the woman and tears started to flow. In an instant, I just knew that she must have lost a precious child, and my suspicions were confirmed when she told me that she had indeed had a son who had died just before his second birthday. She told me that as much as she loved her daughter it was hard not to think about her departed son. And then she dropped the bombshell. Her son's name had been Charlie.

At the next meeting the woman seemed a whole lot happier. She came up to me afterwards and told me that most of the mums at the group knew about her tragedy and none of them knew what to say so they tended to avoid her, but my coming up and introducing myself like that had really helped break the ice. She also couldn't stop thinking that perhaps her son was sending her a message through my son's name mix-up.

Perhaps this has happened to you at some point in your life? You meet someone, and without having any previous knowledge of them you suddenly know things about them. Trust your instinct when this happens. It could well be that you have a very special part to play in helping that person see the light. You may not be able to say or do anything except offer them your time and your empathy, but remember that empathy is a powerful force for good in the world.

To return to the theme of intuition saving lives, these next two stories will almost certainly send shivers down your spine. They did for me. Let's begin with Paula's story:

Dream vacation

It was November 2004 and I was going to book a holiday with my husband in Thailand. It was the dream vacation we had talked about for years, but with our tenth wedding anniversary looming the time just felt right. My husband also had plenty of holiday leave to take and I was between jobs so I went to the travel agent's to make my booking. When I got there though I started to feel a bit dizzy and thought I was going to get one of my migraines so I went back home. The migraine never came so the next day I went back. This time there was such a long queue that I decided to wait until the following day. The following day my car wouldn't start so I couldn't go and then the day after that I slipped and broke my ankle. I am a bit of a superstitious person so I decided that the powers-that-be didn't want me to go inside that travel agent. My husband suggested booking online, so that evening I tried to book, but didn't get very far because, and this I find hard to explain, it just didn't 'feel right' any more.

Eventually we decided to postpone our holiday plans and stay at home for Christmas. On Boxing Day morning when we woke up we found out about the tsunami that had killed hundreds of thousands. I truly believe that if I hadn't listened to my feelings we might have been there, and it's anyone's guess what our fate might have been.

And following on with Robin's:

Nice and slow

I was sitting at some traffic lights waiting for them to turn green when I just knew that I had to do things slower than I normally do. Cars revved up behind me because the lights had turned amber but I didn't want to hurry. I knew I had to take my time. Even when the lights turned green I edged forward slowly, which wasn't easy to do with cars hooting angrily behind. I had just edged gradually past the lights when a car sped from over a bridge to my right and drove in front of me at what must have been eighty miles an hour. It was terrifying but because I wasn't driving quickly I was able to do an emergency stop without causing an accident. If I had driven off quickly, either my car or one of the cars behind me would have collided with that car.

When I think of all the accidents that happen every day, and how much my life has benefited from developing and learning to trust my inner voice, I can't help but imagine what a safer world it might be if everyone became more intuitive – more in touch with their inner angel. If any of the people in the stories above had challenged and overridden their instincts, not tuned into their feelings and thoughts, their stories would have turned our very differently. I guess my message here is simple: listen to your inner voice. It knows things. The voices of goodness, reason and hope are within you. And the more you listen the more you will hear the voices of heavenly angels pressing their lips to your inner ear, speaking to you in the fine air of your intuition.

Sometimes your intuition may manifest in what is known as a premonition, a glimpse of the future or a situation where you know something is going to happen without any concrete evidence to support it. The two previous stories touched on this, because both the people involved had a gut feeling or sense of foreboding and this probably saved their lives. For the people in the next couple of stories the experience goes way beyond foreboding. In both instances the future actually seemed to play out for them in their mind. Let's begin with Kelsey's story.

Shocked to the core

I had this really vivid dream and it shocked me to the core. I dreamt I was being told by my doctor that I had only weeks to live because my bowel cancer had spread to my liver. It was horrible and I woke up really scared.

At first I tried to dismiss the dream as I was really busy working overseas and just didn't have time to go to the doctor, but when I returned home my secretary asked me if I wanted to take a company medical this year. I'd had one the year before so would have declined but my dream had frightened me and I thought it was better to be safe than sorry. You probably know what happens next and you are right. The early stages of bowel cancer were detected. My doctor told me that if I'd waited any longer – or not had my medical this year – my chances of full recovery would not have been so strong.

I have no doubt that dream saved my life. I was fully intending to skip my medical because it wasn't compulsory at my age and because I was so busy at the time. It was only because of that dream that I decided to have the medical. How can you explain that?

Katy's premonition didn't save her life, but she believes it spoke to her about her future.

The sweet little voice

I'd been trying to have a baby for five years so when I got pregnant with Mary you can imagine how blessed I felt. My joy turned to panic, though, when Mary was born premature and came into this world weighing just three pounds. Because she was so small, Mary's organs were not developed and we knew that the first weeks of her life would be a struggle between life and death.

At seven days old Mary became very ill. The only way to save her was a major operation that could take the better part of a day. Jack (my partner) and I clung to each other as the hours ticked away for what seemed like for ever. Twelve or so hours later we both fell asleep, feeling drained.

I woke up with an incredible feeling of alertness and strong, clear memories of a dream I had had. In my dream I had seen myself asleep and a little girl leaning over me. I couldn't see her face because in my dream I was watching everything from behind and I just saw that it was a little blonde girl. Then I heard the little girl say in a sweet little voice with a slight lisp, 'Wake up, Mummy. I'm ready to see you now.'

The voice woke me up and I nudged Jack and told him what I had heard. He told me I was just dreaming. I settled back into his shoulder. I didn't sleep. I just stayed there feeling completely relaxed and confident everything would be OK.

About a minute later a doctor came into the waiting room and told us that Mary was doing fine. To this day I am convinced that the voice I heard in my dream was Mary's. I am certain because Mary is a now six years old and I hear that sweet little voice with the lovely lisp every day.

This next premonition story stands out because it didn't occur in a dream, which is normally the case. Florence, whose story follows on below, was wide awake.

Eyes wide open

This happened to me years ago, in the summer of 1990. I remember it as clearly as if it happened yesterday. It was a Sunday and I got up late. I got dressed and started to brush my teeth. As I was standing in the bathroom and looking in the mirror, a cold shiver went up and down my spine as I had a vision of a blue bus crashing into a motorcycle on a mountain road. The bus tried to swerve but failed and toppled over to one side. I could hear people crying and glass breaking. I even tasted blood my mouth. In an instant the vision in the mirror vanished and I saw my own reflection again. I also saw that I had bitten my tongue and it was bleeding slightly.

I had never experienced anything like this before. I wondered if it might have something to do with the alcohol I had drunk the night before so I dismissed it and forgot about it almost straightaway. It was a strange sensation but it had no relation to anything in my life so I didn't think any more about it, until a year later when I was on vacation with my then boyfriend in Spain.

It was the fifth day of our holiday and we decided to see the sights and go on a coach trip. My boyfriend booked the coach the day before and I was looking forward to it. But when I saw the coach I instantly remembered the vision I had had in my bathroom mirror. The coach was eerily similar. I didn't dare tell my boyfriend because it was early days in our relationship and I didn't want to scare him away, so I told him I had a headache and would have to go back to the hotel. I acted all faint so he would come back with me. I didn't want him boarding that coach.

That evening we watched the local news and heard about a coach crash on the mountain involving a motorbike. Twelve people were killed and dozens were injured, including the driver, who also lost his life. It was the very same blue coach we would have been on. My boyfriend was speechless and even now, all these years later, I still can't believe it myself but I am telling you it is all true. Some may say it is just a coincidence, but it was a coincidence that saved my life. My only regret is that I didn't have the courage to warn those poor people who lost their lives, but even if I had told them I don't think they would have believed me and I think they would have got on the coach all the same.

I've had a few other visions since then, but nothing as significant and life-saving as that one. It looks like it was a one-off. I'm not with my boyfriend any more but we still keep in touch. The bond created by such a close shave is a powerful one.

Kerryanne didn't have a premonition or a vision of the future, but from reading her wonderful and dramatic story below it is clear that her guardian angel gave her mind a powerful jolt.

An angel on my side

On 15 February 2009 my friend (at the time) and I had a gig. She was singing and I worked her equipment. I'm a vocalist and lyricist so I love music and didn't mind helping out a friend. After the gig we had a little drink and then went to a cousin's party. My friend became a bit argumentative so I decided to call a taxi and get us home. We got back and she went to bed. I decided to fall asleep downstairs as she was a bit drunk.

I fell asleep and then suddenly woke up, which is quite unusual for me ... I was surrounded by flames! I thought my mate would have woken up too and gone outside, and I managed to get to the front door and shout for her. I couldn't see her so I ran upstairs. I got to the third stair from the top but couldn't get to her as the smoke from the fire was hot and my feet were burning on the stairs. I ran back outside screaming, 'HELP, HELP, FIRE!' I was falling into fences as the carbon monoxide had just been a bit much for my body to handle.

I managed to run on adrenaline from door to door to try and get help. The fifth door was opened by a man. I told him about the fire and my friend still inside and screamed for help. The man's wife immediately phoned emergency services. She was shouting, ' What can I do to help you?' I replied, 'I'm burning, please help ... cold water!' I had to run upstairs in their house with burned feet and try to get myself into a bath of cold water. Eventually the paramedics came and they told me my friend was out of the house and on her way to hospital. Only then did I fall unconscious. I was in hospital a total of four weeks and had to have a skin graft done from my left shoulder right to my fingertips. I was burnt on my feet, legs, both arms, head, face and chest. Why did I survive? ... Because my guardian angel saved me by waking me up!

The fire brigade told me they didn't understand why both of us were still alive or how I'd woken up because normally with carbon monoxide it poisons you and knocks you out. They said the sofa I'd fallen asleep on went up in flames that were 600 degrees alone. I strongly believe I wasn't meant to die that day and my guardian angel most definitely saved my life by waking me up.

Now I am a music and sound production student at one of the best colleges in Scotland. I love it: that accident made me realise how short life is and that if you really want to do something you can do it ... especially if you have an angel on your side.

In addition to sudden intuitive warnings, dreams and premonitions, another way divine communications can fill your thoughts is when you lose something significant or important to you, like a wallet or purse, or car keys or a treasured family keepsake and you suddenly just know where to find it. In much the same way you might be struggling to remember something or someone important and then seemingly out of nowhere the name, answer or information you need just pops into your mind. Or perhaps you woke up one morning and knew something related to the news without having any prior knowledge of it.

All these are well-reported examples of divine communications through your thought processes that you may not have noticed before, but perhaps one of the most common and hard to dismiss or ignore – and certainly the one I receive the most correspondence about – is when a deceased loved one enters your thoughts, and when they do you 'just know' they are more alive than ever and still close to you. As always it is best to explain with a real-life example, a story sent to me by Polly.

Heartache

I miss my husband more than anything in the entire world. He died seventeen years ago and there isn't a day that goes past when my heart doesn't ache for him. In the first months and years I longed to hear from him, but I never sensed him around me. It wasn't until my son, our son, left home to go to college last year that I got the breakthrough my heart had been aching for.

I missed my son terribly and fell into a dark depression. One night I was lying in my bed feeling wretched and alone when I thought of my husband and in that instant I knew he was with me. This sounds crazy but I knew he was still alive in my heart and in my thoughts. I asked him why he had taken so long to let me know he was still here and I realised that I'd been wrapped up with my son and hadn't needed him before.

That reassurance gave me a huge amount of comfort when I needed it the most. I felt incredibly loved and blessed. Until then I had always had my son to distract me from my grief, life had been so busy raising him, but the biggest challenge for me was facing life alone for the first time without my son. Suddenly, everything made perfect sense to me. I knew that just as my son was alive, but not living at home any more with me, so my husband was alive, but not living on earth with me. Since that night I can honestly say I have never felt alone.

Zak also never feels alone. Here's his story.

Looking out for me

My twin brother died when I was fourteen years old. He had always had a weak heart and it gave out on him. Sometimes when I was growing up I would feel like a part of me was missing, but a series of experiences, which continue to this day, have convinced me otherwise.

I'm convinced that he visits me whenever things aren't going well for me.

It happened the first time when I was sixteen. Mum and Dad divorced and I felt wretched. I missed my brother so badly because only he would have been able to understand what I was going through. At first I just withdrew into myself, basically stopped talking to anyone, but then I woke up one morning and realised this wasn't the way ahead for me. I thought of my brother and how it was up to me to live for the both of us now. I'm nearly forty now and there have been many other times since – school exams, getting a job, splitting from my wife – when I have felt low and retreated into my shell, but then something happens and I just start to pull myself together. It is like I just know I can cope. I'm not confused and despondent any more. I know what needs to be done to help me move forward.

It always begins with me thinking of my brother and what he would think of me. Then I get this warm comforting sensation and the stress flows out of me. It feels as if someone is giving me a great big bear hug and I think that someone is my brother in spirit looking out for me. I think he does it because he loves me and because he wants me to do all the things in life that he never got the chance to do.

Mediums often tell me loved ones in spirit are available to us every time we think about them. They are only ever a thought away and completely aware of our thoughts and feelings about them. Death does not end a relationship; indeed it can enhance it because there is no longer any judgement on either side and we can communicate our truest thoughts and feelings to our loved ones, anytime, anywhere.

In the chapters that follow you'll see that in addition to entering your thoughts there are many other ways that departed loved ones can communicate with you. For now though, I'll leave you with the powerful, and potentially life-transforming, thought that loved ones in spirit are alive in your mind and in your heart. The dead don't leave us, they just change form. And, whenever you think of them and send them loving thoughts, love and comfort from above will come right back to you.

Just knowing

You may have noticed in this chapter that I used the words 'just knowing' and 'just know' several times. Intuition just knows what is right for us, but when we grow up and leave childhood innocence and trust behind we allow layers of fear and self-doubt to creep in and we stop trusting it. We start forgetting that we are spirits in human form and stop trusting that we will be given what we need. In the words of Albert Einstein, who said it far better than I ever could: 'The intuitive mind is a sacred gift and the rational mind is a faithful servant. We have created a society that honours the servant and has forgotten the gift.' It doesn't have to be this way though. With a little patience and persistence we can all reconnect with our intuition, our very own channel to the divine within us and all around us.

I'm no expert, but from all I have researched and experienced over the years, one of the best ways to cultivate your intuition is to experience silence. So take time out each day to be quiet. It doesn't have to be long – five or ten minutes will do. Don't try to think during this period of silence, just listen and be. Creativity is an expression of your spirit and goes hand-in-hand with intuitive guidance, so you may want to spend time writing, drawing, dancing, singing, listening to music or doing anything that helps you relax and unwind. Walking in the countryside can also help clear your mind and journal writing can make it easier for you to hear your own thoughts. And finally, at all times, keep your mind as open to new possibilities as possible. Be curious about everything and everyone. Keep asking yourself questions and trust that your angels will send you the answers.

But how do you know if an idea is divinely inspired or not?

I've been asked this question a lot, but I never tire of answering it because each time I do my understanding deepens further. Here's where I am so far. First of all, divinely inspired intuition is typically repetitive and persistent. It won't be a flash in the pan that illogically darts around and changes direction. It will remain unchanged and stick with you over time. Second, it is always positive, uplifting and life-enhancing and motivated by a desire to improve a situation not just for yourself, but for others too. It excites and energises you. Thirdly, when you know something intuitively you just know it, without a lot of words to explain it, even if that knowing appears illogical. If the thoughts in your mind are full of 'waffle' and endless explanations and justifications, they are not angel-inspired. What I'm talking about here is a quiet knowing of the truth.

And finally, divine insight is always gentle and non-judgemental. If the voices in your head clatter around harshly and tell you that you are a loser, or that you always give up, you can't do what it takes, it isn't your angels talking but your fear and self-doubt. Your angels might, however, tell you, in gentle whisper-like tones, that something doesn't feel right, that this isn't the right thing for you or that it is time for you to move on, change direction and find what works better for you.

As the next chapter shows, in some instances there may be no words or no thoughts at all, just a strong awareness of what you need to know or do, just a powerful feeling or vision that drives you forward, just a quiet knowing and certainty that you are hearing the voice of truth ...

CHAPTER 4

Messages from Heaven

> *Let us be silent that we may hear the whisper of
> God.*
>
> Ralph Waldo Emerson

Of course, it's not just through words, sounds, dreams and
thoughts that angels can send us messages. They can also speak
to us through our physical and emotional feelings, as well as
through visions and images. As always, the best way to make all
this come to life for you is with real stories, so let's leap ahead
with this one sent to me by Sophie.

A strange and familiar feeling

When my mum died I just couldn't accept it. After Dad left it had
always been just me and her. She was my best friend and my only comfort. Suddenly, I was all alone. Eight months after her funeral I still
didn't want to sort through her possessions because it felt too final. I
guess you could say I was having trouble with the grieving process.

I felt totally bereft and there was nothing to fill the void. My mum always believed in angels. I never really took to the idea and when she was alive and told me she believed her parents were watching over in spirit, I used to find it a creepy idea that we are always being watched.

Anyway, one day I tried to pluck up the courage to sort out her things. I went into her room and it still smelled of her. It was all too much and I sat down on the bed and started to cry. When I looked up the first thing I saw was Mum's guardian angel figurine. As I said, she had been into all that kind of stuff. It wasn't for me. I was never religious or spiritual, although I would call myself an ethical person with a concern for the well-being of others. That's why what happened next surprised me so much. I couldn't take my eyes off the angel figurine. It was like they were stuck there, if you know what I mean, and the more I stared the more it felt as if the room was filled with the warmth of sunlight. It was blissful.

I realised in that moment that my mum was in that room with me. I couldn't see her, but I could feel her. I found myself saying hello to her and I could feel her saying hello back to me. It was incredible and it was an experience I hadn't expected and certainly wasn't conditioned for. It was if Mum was saying, 'OK, you can't see me but I am here with you in another plane or dimension, but wherever I am, I am still strongly connected to you. I'm always here if you need me.'

The experience was tremendously healing and reassuring and oddly familiar. After that I was able to let go of a lot of my grief and sense of loss. I was significantly better. I've done a lot of reading about angels since and it means the world to me to know that mine was not an isolated incident. My best friend told me that it was simply a natural part of the healing process, but that explanation doesn't feel right.

In the past I never used to trust my feelings, but now they are the guiding force in my life. I can't understand why I used to find the idea of angels alarming. Now it is the most comforting feeling in the world to know that the people you have loved and lost will always be there for you. And whenever I feel down or sad, I pick up that angel figurine or simply say the word angel in my mind and often the same thing happens – I feel Mum standing right beside me.

In this next compelling and moving story, sent to me via email by Carla, gut feelings that an experience is spiritual, and a powerful sense that the loving bond created between two people can transcend the boundaries of time, place and even death, also feature strongly.

Soul mate

I had known my fiancé, Ian, for over seven years. We dated for a brief time when I was fourteen and he was my first love. Like many teenage romances ours didn't last, but long after we split I still cared deeply about him. I had a child from another relationship and raised her by myself, with the support of my family and closest friends.

Three years after I lost contact with Ian, when my daughter had just turned two, I had a horrific nightmare about Ian driving his car off the edge of a concrete ledge into the sea. At one point I was in the car with him as he was driving towards the verge. I could hear his thoughts, although he couldn't see me sitting beside him in the passenger seat. Listening to his thoughts, I was fixed to the seat unable to move, but not really wanting to. I can't remember the exact words but it was something like this . . . 'I can't take this in any more, they don't care about me. They hate me and don't even want me around. This life hurts so much I can physically feel the pain. I love them but they hate me.' I was shocked when at one point I felt a small reference to myself in his thoughts. And the feeling he was having when he thought of me was the love right deep down in my own heart, but it was also his feeling.

I woke up terrified, unable to sleep. I was frightened for him. I didn't have a way to contact him any more. I tried ringing his family's home phone, but the number had changed. Shaken and worried, I went back to sleep and for three nights afterwards my sleep was disturbed by constant variations of his suicide. Sometimes he was in a dark wooden room that looked like an old jail cell as he overdosed on medicine and I watched him retch in pain before having a fit and dying. Others were of him at a bridge with a backpack weighed down with stones. All of these nightmares were so incredibly detailed and lifelike that I felt I was genuinely watching him, but however hard I tried to make contact he could not hear or see me, except in that split second before he died.

On the third night I woke up soaked in my own sweat. My sheets were soaked through too and I was pale and shaking and felt sick. It was morning. I got up and made my daughter breakfast in a sleep-deprived daze but all the time the dream replayed over and over in my mind. I realised that somewhere in my mind there was a picture of a number! It was clear and I could remember it. I wrote it down instantly, worried I would forget it.

Without hesitation I dialled the number and to my complete amazement it rang. A deep voice that I instantly knew answered. I blurted out why I had called. Ian wasn't very responsive and when the call had finished I worried that I had really unsettled him, but a week or so later he texted me saying he had attempted to take his life about a year before in his brother's car. He also told me he still had a love letter I had written him from years back. We met up and within months were living together and then within the year we were engaged.

I could tell he had a lot of problems mentally and in the time we lived together his alcohol dependency was obvious. He didn't need it every day but he did need it on difficult days, so we organised house parties with friends every two weeks so he knew how long he had to wait till he could drink. Our method of control worked well for him but then after we had been together for two years we were in his car when it skidded out of control on black ice. The car had always been his pride and joy. He had saved for years to get it and when it was written off he was heartbroken and things spiralled downwards from then on. His mental problems got progressively worse and it was obvious he was in need of serious help. He would argue for hours for no reason he could remember. The smallest problem would stress him out for days on end and he lost all patience with my daughter when he had always been an amazingly loving and doting dad to her.

His mood shifts were too upsetting for me to deal with and I didn't want my daughter to witness any more trauma so we split up. He moved back in with his parents because he refused to talk to anyone professional about his problems. I just felt powerless to help him. All I could do was urge him to see a doctor but he refused. In December 2009, a week after begging me to take him back, he took his own life, in a place special to us because it was where we used to go in the summer on holidays.

If leaving him had been traumatic, hearing the news of his death was devastating and I was on the verge of a nervous breakdown. I didn't think he would do that to himself and to us and everyone who knew and loved him. Worse still, his family and friends told me it was my fault for leaving him, but I know that is not what he thought because he told me so in a letter he posted through the door the night he went missing.

I had a deep need to see the place where he died so one morning I went there with my mum and a friend. Even though it was close to Christmas, it was a warm and sunny day. After a while it started to rain gently. My heart was breaking as I looked at the broken glass that was probably left behind from where he had crashed his car. I stood where he would have been in the car and cried but then my mum and friend both said, 'Look.' I looked up and saw a small yet beautiful rainbow right above us. It didn't start or stop anywhere. It just lingered high in the sky above us.

I cried and laughed and in that moment I knew in my gut, in my heart, that he was OK and this was his sign to tell me. A few months later my friends and I went for a meal in the place where he proposed to me to say our farewells. (His mother had not wanted me to attend the funeral.) During the meal the same vocalist was singing who had performed the night Ian had proposed to me, and he sang the same songs – 'Lady in Red' and 'My Girl'.

We ate and cried our way through the evening and I smiled inside, remembering how we had always danced to 'My Girl', and how Ian would sing along to it in my ear, when suddenly in the empty seat beside me I felt him. I actually felt him place his arm around my shoulders. The feeling of his arms around me was so unexpected I felt startled and in a flash the sensation disappeared. Once I had calmed down I thanked him from the bottom of my heart for giving me the chance to feel his arms around me one more time. It was something I never thought I would feel again.

I have always believed in angels and now that 'spiritual hug' experience has strengthened my belief even further. My daughter believes that her daddy – because in the brief time he was with us that is what he meant to her – is an angel who is watching over her and keeping her safe. At night she tells me that she can feel his presence. I don't think I'll ever understand why he took his life, but what I do know is that he sent me a rainbow that day and he put his arms around me that evening. On both those occasions I felt as if I would somehow cope with the loss. For now I have my beautiful daughter and my wonderful friends and family. They are enough for me until the day I get to meet my angel soul mate in eternity.

There is just so much to take in with this story, so many painful issues, but also wonderful themes, that you may need to read it a number of times, as I did. When there is a strong bond between people, for example between mother and child or between lovers, they can often sense or even actually feel each other's struggles, and this was clearly the case for Carla. I struggled at first to know where to place Carla's story as it features angel messages delivered through premonitions, dreams and angel signs, all of which are discussed in more detail elsewhere, but the reason I eventually decided to place it here is that it concludes powerfully with the feeling of being hugged by someone invisible.

Do you remember Danusia and her wonderful lucky number

story a few pages back? In her account below, she also describes this sensation of being warmly embraced.

Warm embrace

In February 2009 my dear late mother had been in hospital for an operation to remove a lump from her bowel. She did not have a very good time there, suffering an infection, bad treatment from a nurse and enduring a minor stroke. But once home she was on the slow road to recovery. She lived alone and was very independent, but this operation had left her weak and tired. Fortunately, we are a large family and there was plenty of help at hand on a daily basis for anything that she wanted us to do for her.

But on Monday 11 May 2009, I had taken her to see her doctor as she had been complaining of dizziness every time she blew her nose. The doctor gave her a thorough examination and gave her the all-clear. On Thursday 14 May 2009 I was out working in the morning (I am a driving instructor) but my mother was on my mind all the time and I was feeling rather irritable and in a bad mood, but couldn't quite put my finger on why!

I had just dropped my student off after her lesson when my mobile rang. I could not answer it as I was driving and by the time I had pulled over whoever it was had rung off, but as I looked at my phone I could see it was a missed call from my brother. My brother used to sit with my mother every Thursday and therefore I instinctively knew something had happened to her. I didn't bother ringing him back. I just drove as fast as I could to Mum's house, which thankfully was only a very short drive from where I was. I ran into the house to find my brother on the phone to the ambulance service and my mother in a heap on the floor; she had suffered a massive stroke. I knew there and then that the feelings I had been having all morning were a message to get to my mother, and I had not listened to them.

At hospital Mum made only a very minor recovery, managing to tell me that she had tried to telephone me as she knew she didn't feel right, but could only remember my home number not my mobile and, of course, there was nobody at my house, because I was out driving. The phone was found on the floor next to her. She was in the hospital for one year and sadly, but a blessing, she passed away a year to the day from a massive stroke, 14 May 2010. I miss her dearly, and feel an element of guilt and sadness that I didn't listen to that little voice in my head. I won't be ignoring it again!

Then last night as I wrote this story out for you on a piece of paper ready to send to you today via email, I went to bed feeling upset and guilty again, but in the early hours I was woken by an almost suffocating embrace, like wings wrapped tightly around me; I felt warm and secure and at peace. I did not open my eyes, but mentally said thank you as I drifted back off to sleep.

I have always had a belief in 'something else being out there' without realising exactly what, but now after that experience I have an almighty love of and belief in the guardian angels that look out for us, and also family members who have passed who watch over us.

Feeling guilty when a loved one passes over, perhaps because you weren't there or because you didn't get a chance to say goodbye properly is a very common experience, but from the letters I have received, and my own experience, I am convinced that loved ones in spirit can and do send messages of comfort and reassurance, as was the case for Carla and Danusia in their stories above. I am also convinced that the aspiring angel inside our loved ones may sometimes choose to slip away alone because it is easier for spirit to leave without the presence of loved ones willing them to stay.

In the months and years that followed my mum's death twenty years ago I never stopped berating myself for not being with her when she died. I hated myself for not sensing that her time was nearly up and for throwing myself into my career when I should have been with her. Whenever I begged for a sign of forgiveness from her and there was only silence I was convinced that she was angry with me for deserting her, for not being with her in her hour of need and letting her die alone. In my heart of hearts I knew that my mother could never hate me but I couldn't let go of my guilt. The pain came gushing back to me in sporadic waves. Just when I thought I had come to terms with my regret, it would come back with such a force it would knock me sideways. And never was the pain more intense than on my daughter's first birthday. My mother had always longed for grandchildren but had died before I got married and had them.

With about an hour to go before the party guests arrived, I stared at my daughter's birthday cake and thought about my mother's final lonely moments before she died. I hadn't been there to hold her hand. I kept my hands busy by tidying the house and making preparations but this didn't keep my mind busy and I remembered my mother crying the last few times I left her. Why hadn't I stayed with her? I tried to pull myself together but the memory of my mother's tearful and disappointed face overwhelmed me. My grief and hurt became so intense that I found it hard to breathe. I walked outside, hoping that a gust of fresh air would help release the tension inside.

When I walked outside I noticed that it was a cold but beautiful afternoon with the promise of a warmer evening ahead. The sun was shining brightly in the sky and as I looked up I closed my tearful eyes for a moment to escape the glare. The sight that met my gaze when I opened my eyes was breathtaking. There in the centre of the sky was a cloud in the shape of an angel. It was perfect in every detail, especially the wings, which seemed to spread right from the top of the angel's head to the bottom of its billowing gown. The angel's hands were folded as if in prayer. What made the cloud even more remarkable was that it was stationary and clear white, whereas the clouds around it looked like they were moving.

I'd often read about angels appearing in the guise of clouds, but this was the first time I had seen one for myself. I knew then that my mum had forgiven me. I also knew that she had never been angry with me in the first place. A deep sensation of warmth, happiness and peace filled me and the burden of my guilt that had weighed heavily in my heart all these years lifted. Here at last was the sign of forgiveness I had been looking for. The cloud remained so clear for such a long time that it will be forever imprinted in my fondest memories.

Deep sensations of warmth and happiness are a common way for angels and loved ones in spirit to connect with us. Also common is a sudden and unexpected surge of euphoria or bliss coming direct from your heart. Ross writes about this experience below.

Coming out

Not long ago I discovered that I am gay. It was a shocking discovery for me, especially as I have never fantasised about men or had any relationship with them beyond friendship. I don't often daydream but when I do it usually involves me and a woman, so you must be wondering how I discovered I was gay.

It all started a few months ago when I caught up with an old school friend. He had just got married and his wife was expecting her first child. We had been best mates at school and regularly kept in touch so I kind of joked, saying that I wasn't ready to be a godfather. My friend didn't laugh and told me that he would love me to be his child's godfather but his wife had a problem with me because I was thirty-five and lived alone, so she thought I had to be gay. It wasn't just her who thought this about me either – most of my friends did too.

Let me get this straight. I am gay because I live alone and don't go chasing after women. I can't figure out when people started thinking of me this way but it seems I am out of the closet, even though I missed the moment when it happened.

My first reaction was panic and I went on a campaign to prove to my friends I wasn't gay. I went to a club and took a girl home. The next night I went to the club with the intention of taking a different girl home but it just felt empty so I spent most of my time at the bar drinking and drinking. I drank so much in fact that I can't remember much of what happened except that when I woke up with a splitting headache I was in bed with another guy.

Turns out nothing happened between me and him. His name is Mickey, by the way, and he's a great guy. We just got chatting at the bar and wound up at his place, where I passed out. Yes, Mickey is gay, but he didn't try it on or anything. He's great company, though, and I've been hanging out with him ever since because he is so well read and cultured and always has something interesting, funny or positive to say.

You can just imagine the reaction of my friends when they found out about my new friend. That was it. To them I was gay. I tried to tell them this wasn't necessarily the case, and Mickey already had a boyfriend, but it was like bashing my head against a brick wall. It started to make me really unhappy and I began to drink a lot to help me cope with it all.

One night after a dinner party with my friends I drank way too much. When I was walking – or should I say stumbling – home I fell over and really scraped my knees and arms. It hurt like hell and I found it hard to get up. All of a sudden, I started to cry because my friends shouldn't have let me go home on my own in this disorientated state. I realised as I scrambled around on the pavement that they weren't really friends to me at all and that they had no right to make assumptions about me. If they were friends they would love me for the person I was.

At the exact same moment, I felt a pair of strong arms wrap around me and I was gently helped up into a standing position. I turned around to say thank you, but there was no one there. It was incredible and I might have put it down to my drunken state, but when I stood up I found that I had lost all my shakiness and disorientation. My knees and elbows were still sore and scraped from my fall but my head had never felt so clear. I wasn't drunk. I felt wonderful, blissful in fact.

I started to run and half expected to fly off the ground, so intensely alive and happy did I feel.

My life changed for ever after that moment. I'm still not sure if my guardian angel saved me that night, just as I'm not really sure if I am gay or straight. I suspect I'm a bit of both, but it doesn't matter because I know when the time is right for me to decide my guardian angel will be there to support me every step of the way, with whatever decision I make. My guardian angel loves me just the way I am.

As for my friends, apart from one or two, I don't see them any more. I am making a whole new set of friends – people who don't judge me or make assumptions about me or try to put me in a box, because I don't think I will ever fit into any kind of box. I'm a real square peg and proud of it. I'd rather have just one friend, like Mickey, who builds me up, instead of thirty so-called 'friends' who try to pull me down.

Another comforting angel experience is the feeling that someone or something invisible is actually hugging you, stroking your hair or gently squeezing your hand. Often these experiences are dismissed as wishful thinking or a form of self-comfort, but if that is the case why doesn't everyone who is grieving or in distress report this sensation? Also, the experiences tend to take a person completely by surprise, happening when they least expect it. This was certainly the case for Martin.

Holding the right hand

I wasn't brought up in a religious family and I haven't brought up my children to be religious either. I suppose you could say I believe in the power of goodness and love, but until two weeks ago I would have said that we are born, we live and we die and that is it – curtains. I was a realist. I don't think I could say that about myself now. I'm probably not making much sense so I better get on with my story.

Two weeks ago I was walking my five-year-old and six-year-old sons to school. Since I was made redundant six months ago I've done that every morning and afternoon and I can honestly say it is the happiest part of my day. There are quite a few dads doing the school run these days and on that particular morning we found ourselves walking along the road with Paul, another dad who also has two sons at the school. My sons flew in the direction of his sons and we ended up walking behind them chatting.

With all the chatting and playing going on we must have walked slower than usual because when I glanced at my watch I realised we were running late. We were coming to a main road and needed to cross in front of a parked school bus that had yellow lights flashing. In my haste I assumed cars would stop when they saw the flashing lights and I didn't look carefully enough and proceeded to cross with my sons holding my hands. We were in a straight line, with me in the middle of them, walking in front of the bus but then something happened. I felt my younger son, who was holding my right hand, pull me back a few steps. As he pulled me back it felt like life had gone into slow motion. Then a car flew past a few inches ahead of us at about forty miles an hour and life fast forwarded back to normal. I turned to watch the car speed by.

My heart was beating so fast because I knew if we had stepped in front of that car my younger son, indeed all three of us, would almost certainly have been killed. But I haven't got to the most astonishing part of my story yet. When I turned to look at the car speeding by I noticed that both my sons were standing on my LEFT-hand side – my younger was holding my left hand and my elder was holding my younger son's hand. Later when I asked Paul he told me that he really thought I would be hit by the car because I had been standing in the line of fire with my two sons on my left-hand side.

The question is, who or what tugged at my right hand that day and stopped me walking in front of that car because I wasn't looking or thinking? It all happened in a split second but it felt like much longer than that, like a slow-motion video. When I asked my sons about it they said they thought it was me pulling them back, but I know this isn't what happened. My guardian angel held my hand and saved all our lives. I know now that there is another world out there watching over us and I feel incredibly warm, supported and loved because of that knowledge.

In her story below, Clare also felt warm, supported and loved after a visit from her guardian angel.

Good news

It took a while for me to meet the love of my life. I met Jim when I was forty-three and he was fifty-three. We both had divorces behind us, but there was an instant connection between us. We fell head over heels in love. He was such good news for me. He loved me when I was happy and when I was feeling sad. He didn't want me to change for him. He just loved me for being me. I was an incredibly lucky woman.

Although Jim had three sons from his previous marriage and wasn't that keen on starting another family, he sensed how important it was for me, and two years after we got married, at the grand old age of forty-six, I gave birth to a beautiful baby girl. My happiness was complete, but then my world turned upside down.

On 19 May 1999, Jim died. He had an aneurism. I went into shock. I didn't even want to see my daughter and my sister had to step in to look after her. Without Jim I didn't want to be a mother. He had been my world. For several months I went to the darkest place imaginable, a living hell. On the night before my daughter's second birthday I felt so sad and disgusted with myself that I couldn't be a mother to her that I decided to end my life. Not really thinking clearly I remember heading towards some railway track close to my house. It was a really cold evening and all I could think about was Jim and how I would soon be with him.

I was getting close to the tracks when suddenly I felt two very strong, warm arms go around my waist. I was so surprised that I stood perfectly still. I was scared to move because I didn't want the sensation to end. When Jim had been alive, whenever I felt sad or upset or in need of comfort he used to hold me in this way, gently rocking me. The pressure of the hands got stronger and I felt myself being swayed gently from side to side. Eventually I couldn't resist the temptation to turn around. Jim wasn't there.

The feeling of being supported and loved and rocked like a baby stayed with me for several hours, but the most important thing is that the experience made me realise that there was a baby who needed me to rock and comfort her in the same way. My daughter had already lost a father, losing me would be even more devastating. Jim's comforting words and arms had always calmed and reassured me and I knew then that he was urging me to do the same for our beloved daughter. He made a special effort to reach out to me when I really needed it, and it was up to me now to make a special effort too for our daughter. That night I chose life and I chose love.

My daughter is nearly thirteen now and asking a lot of questions about her father. I tell her everything I can remember. I also tell her that he is very much alive in me and in her.

A comparable theme of comfort, love and reassurance runs through Debbi's intriguing story below.

Good night

I've never been a good sleeper but after the summer of 2005 I got full blown insomnia. I think it started after I had a really silly argument with my then boyfriend on the phone one evening. He got me really upset and I couldn't sleep because I was replaying the conversation over and over again in my head. Eventually at around three am I crept into the lounge and watched TV until I dozed off. We broke up soon afterwards and I didn't date after that because I was always too tired.

It was always the same. I would head to bed before midnight and lie there tossing and turning and unable to sleep because I found myself getting upset about conversations I had had or things that had happened during the day. Around three am I would be on the sofa watching TV, where I would eventually drift off. I tried everything and sometimes my shopping basket had enough sleeping aids to tranquillise an elephant. Friends and family would send me candles and hypnotherapy tapes. I tried exercise, light therapy, diet change and long baths. You name it, I tried it. Nothing worked. I was desperate for a decent night's sleep but for two years I rarely got one. I existed on three, four hours' sleep a night, tops. I had black circles under my eyes and was constantly moody and tearful.

In January 2007 I was dropping off constantly at work or in one terrible instance at the wheel of my car. My doctor was prescribing me regular sleeping tablets and I stopped working and moved back home with my dad. My life came to a standstill. I was too tired to see any way out. Then, on the evening of 21 January 2007, I fell asleep before midnight for the first time in years and this is how it happened.

It was about nine pm and I was lying on my bed staring at the ceiling. I felt cold so I crawled under the duvet and tried to close my eyes, praying for the miracle of sleep. It didn't happen and soon my eyes were wide open again. I started to think about Dad and how quiet he had been today. I knew he was worried about me, and I wished he didn't have to be. I really wanted to get better for him. As I lay there I felt myself being gently tucked in. I wasn't hallucinating but there was nobody in the room with me. I felt the duvet pull up against my chin and then tuck around my shoulders. It was the most blissful and calming sensation. All the stress and worry fell off me and my eyes became heavy.

I slept for a good fifteen hours – yes fifteen hours – straight that night and I can honestly say I have never had any problems getting to sleep since. When I told my doctor my story I could tell he didn't believe me, but my dad did and I think you will and that's why I decided to get in touch. I really did feel as if someone invisible tucked me in that night. I haven't felt the same sensation since, but it doesn't matter – just thinking about it gives me a warm feeling and helps me relax and unwind and drift off to the land of sleep and dreams.

Just thinking about her own astonishing experience is also a daily source of inspiration for Kathy, and she talks about it below.

Back off

Five years ago when I was fifteen I was walking home from work through the park when I got this uncomfortable feeling. I just knew someone was following me, but it was daylight and the park was fairly busy so I didn't think I had anything to worry about. I walked through the park and then down the road to my house. I started to panic when I realised that the road was empty apart from me. I turned around, worried that I was still being followed, but no one was there. Relieved, I started to walk briskly to my house, but then suddenly from out of nowhere I felt a hand clap over my mouth. Unable to scream and totally powerless, I was dragged back into the trees on the edge of the park. I was old enough to know what was going to happen next.

I tried to struggle and pull myself away but it was pathetic. There was nothing I could do so I just went entirely limp. I could tell this confused him because he started to shout at me and slap my cheeks. He slapped me hard several times but I didn't feel anything. It was as if I had gone numb. Things were happening but I couldn't feel them. All I could feel was a sense of tightness in my head, like someone was knocking on it. It was a bit like being pulled underwater, but I wasn't struggling to breathe. Just then, I felt an unknown force shoot from my head to my body and I awoke from my trance-like state with a sudden jolt, screaming, 'Back off!' It clearly freaked the guy out because he dropped me and stumbled away with his mouth open.

For a few seconds we just stood there staring at each other. I took in every detail of his horrible face and then I bolted right past him back into the road, where a couple were walking by. I ran to them screaming that a man had tried to attack me. Within an hour the police had arrived and I was able to give an extremely accurate picture of my attacker. Three weeks later I was asked to attend an identity parade and I picked him out immediately.

You might have thought that after my ordeal that I would be terrified to walk anywhere alone again and you'd be right. For months afterwards I did get scared and always made sure I had someone else with me, but over time a strange calm descended on me. The more I thought about it the more I realised that some spiritual essence or force had entered my body and saved my life. My guardian angel had intervened and changed not just my life but the way I think about this world and the next.

The feeling of tightness around the head, or the sensation of being pulled underwater, that Kathy mentions is something that other people have written to me or told me about before. I don't have personal experience of it but it does seem to be another way for angels to reach out to us through both physical and emotional feelings.

Kathy also talks about the awareness of someone or something standing behind you. In her story this had a sinister overtone in that she was actually being stalked by a person with ugly intentions, but from my own experience and also from the emails I receive this 'look behind you' sensation – but when you turn around there is no one there – can be a sign that your guardian angel is close by.

My advice if you experience the 'look behind you' sensation is to breathe deeply and stay calm. Of course, you should double-check that you aren't being followed, spied on or in danger, as Kathy was in her story. However, once you have established that you are not in any danger – as is almost always the case – especially when you know you are completely alone, rejoice in the closeness of your guardian angel. Thank your angel for watching over you so intently and for reminding you of the angel's comforting and enduring presence. Use the sensation to open your mind and your heart and ask for divine guidance and inspiration.

If you're still wondering at this point why you haven't heard the voice or felt the touch of an angel, again I urge you to look deep within yourself and find a resonance of something you may have missed before. Look back on your life and think deeply. There must have been times or moments in your life when you had a feeling about something or someone. Perhaps that inner prompting came in a dream or perhaps in the words of someone else or in a sudden flash of intuition. Sometimes you may have acted on these feelings and sometimes you didn't. It could be as simple as the irrational urge to walk a different route and on the way you bump into an old friend. Or perhaps you have a prompting to call a friend and when you do you discover they have been thinking about you. Or perhaps you get an inner prompting to take a different route to the one you were intending to take and then find out later there was an incident or an accident on the route you would have taken.

I'm sure if you look back on your life you will remember something – a whisper, a hint, an echo of something – that you may have not paid attention to before. Perhaps that 'something' is here with you right now as you read this book and perhaps by remembering, reconnecting with or anticipating it, it will turn into a truly decisive moment in your life, when 'something' becomes everything.

It's often the case that simply thinking about the possibility of angels touching your life can change any feelings of uncertainty and loneliness you may have into feelings of certainty and comfort. Our angels and loved ones in spirit are always trying to talk to us through our feelings. You may feel invisible arms wrapping themselves around you, or a sensation of warmth, or invisible lips kissing your cheek. Or perhaps you catch a whiff of lovely flowers or spellbindingly beautiful perfume when there is no blossom or person nearby. Sometimes the sensation is physical and other times it is just a peaceful but powerful sensation that fills you with a sudden surge of euphoria or bliss for no apparent reason. Hold onto these sensations – they are all signs of angelic presence, and remember, if you ever feel afraid, anxious or confused, it is not your angel but your ego doing the talking.

There may be a slight flicker of uncertainty at the strangeness of it all but it will soon pass and be replaced by something positive and reassuring. Remember, true spiritual experiences will always feel safe, warm, loving and inspiring.

Clear seeing

From hearing, feeling or sensing the world of spirit, let's move on now to perhaps the ultimate way for heaven to speak to us – visions. In the bundle of stories that conclude this chapter you'll read about people who believe they have actually seen angels with their eyes wide open. Some people see lights or colours or glimpses of angel wings or just flickers of something in their corners of their eyes, while others see spiritual figures or even full blown celestial beings complete with halo and wings. This story was sent to me by Anne Marie:

Silver angel

This angel experience relates to my mother, Irene. She died in July 2009, aged ninety-three and a half, and this happened several months before she died. She was a very truthful person and would not have said this if it didn't happen to her. She said she was lying in bed in her darkened bedroom, and suddenly there was a flash and two silver angels with long wings were standing by the bed. One was an adult female and the other a female child, about eleven years old. Mum said, 'Oh, you've come for me!' but they didn't speak; there was another flash and they were gone. That was all.

Laura also emailed me about her extraordinary experience.

For ever and always

Back in 2006 I was quite ill, suffering from depression and anxiety, post-traumatic stress disorder and borderline personality disorder. That was the diagnosis anyway. It got to a point where I had a nervous breakdown and needed to go to hospital. Despite my diagnosis I wasn't given any medication to help me cope with my inner demons. I felt like I was in one big black hole and I couldn't escape.

Being stuck in hospital was a living nightmare until one night, 27 March 2009. It was around three am and I was sitting on my bed in my dorm, wide awake trying to block out my demons, when all of a sudden I felt a rush of warmth and love. That love spilled out opposite my bed and poured into the mirror there. In the mirror it appeared as what I can only describe as a beautiful angel with no voice. Her glow was warm and she had a beautiful neon blue and white aura swirling around her – it was like no colour on earth and it bounced around this beautiful angel. Her hair was flowing perfectly. It was so blonde and golden.

Then the most amazing thing happened: this being of light spoke to me not in a physical sense, but on an emotional level. She moved her lips (although there was no physical sound) and said, 'Everything's going to be all right!' She then faded. I was a little sad to see her leave but I knew from that moment on my life would be better for ever. The whole experience must have lasted around thirty minutes.

The next morning I was allowed to return home and slowly but surely my life began to improve. The funny thing is that earlier during the day I had decided to ask God if he could send me a message. So I guess you could say my prayers where well and truly answered. I really do believe in angels and I can feel their presence each and every day. I feel truly blessed to have received such a visit and I do believe this angel saved me and gave me a second chance! I will always be grateful to this angel, for ever and always.

In both these stories the angel vision took the form of a female but this is not always the case, as Jacqueline's story illustrates below.

The monk

My mother's story happened in 1984 when she was very ill with cervical cancer.

One evening when she was between treatments and in her own home she awoke very suddenly and, for what she says was only a few seconds, saw a monk sitting on the end of her bed. He was wearing a brown cassock with his hood up and had piercing eyes that looked right into hers. He didn't smile or say a word but she says she wasn't afraid and felt calm. When he went she felt as if she was in a different bedroom as her wallpaper had a different pattern.

She remembers it so well and wasn't dreaming and wonders if this was an angel. She was very ill at the time, but survived the cancer only to develop lung cancer three months later!

The cancers were both primary cancers and at the time the hospital was trying out new drugs on her and told me that if they didn't work she would live for about three months. If the drugs did work she might still only have a year. She wasn't given this information as they were worried she might not fight it. My mum is almost seventy-seven now and made it through two cancers and has often wondered if through her own prayers to the angel world she has indeed been 'helped'.

Thank you for reading my accounts. I firmly believe that angels are around us helping us in our everyday lives and will never hesitate to ask for help when I need it.

Angels are spiritual beings. They don't have human bodies and are actually neither male nor female. People tend to see them in the way they need to see them, or which makes the most sense to them at the time, so if you have a strong belief that angels should appear in their traditional guise with wings and halo, you are more likely to see them in this way and the same applies to their gender. More and more people today, however, don't have such a fixed idea of what an angel should or should not look like. Perhaps this is due to the move away from conventional religion in recent years. As a result, increasing numbers of people are not seeing angels in their traditional form, but in countless different ways – ways that are unique but always instinctively recognisable as divine to the individual experiencing them.

In this next story, Davina's angel appeared in a way that made perfect sense to her.

Round the clock

When Mum was sixty-seven she had the first of several heart attacks. It was horrible watching her suffer so much. She had always been so independent and now she was totally dependent on my sister and me for everything. It was very tough for me because I had three children to care for but Mum needed round-the-clock care. She did get a home visit twice a day but I could tell it wasn't enough for her. I was torn between love for my mother and my children as both needed me and I didn't know where I should be. I prayed for a miracle and one night I got as close to getting one as you can imagine.

Mum had had a really bad day and I didn't think she should be alone that night so I decided to stay over. I called my husband and said a tearful goodnight to my girls and then settled down to read a book beside Mum's bed. It was obvious to me how relieved Mum was to have my company and I felt so guilty for leaving her in the months previously. Mum drifted off into a peaceful sleep and I must have drifted off too because when I woke up there was a very bright light in my eyes. At first I thought I must have left the light on. I looked up to the clock on Mum's bedroom wall and saw a tiny, bright figure hovering just in front of it. It looked male, but I can't be sure. It had a shiny face and pink cheeks. As I looked at him I felt love in my heart like I have never known before. I felt his love entering my heart. Then he looked at me as if I had startled him. Our eyes met for just a brief moment and then he vanished and I fell asleep again.

The next morning when I woke up I didn't remember my vision at first. It was only when I glanced at the clock to check the time that it all came flashing back. I thought it must be a dream but I know for sure it wasn't. I believe I saw an angel and he came to help my mum. It has been five years since that night and she has not had another heart attack. She still lives alone and I still have to juggle my family with making sure she is OK but, it's hard to explain, I don't feel weighed down any more. I feel able to cope with whatever life throws at me. Also, seeing my angel appear in a clock reminds me just how precious each second of our lives is. I try to remember that whenever I feel stressed. Instead of looking at my watch and feeling anxious because I'm running behind, I take a deep breath and try to stay in the moment. Looking at my watch used to wind me up but now it winds me down.

I just wanted to share my story with you because I know there are a lot of people out there with elderly relatives or loved ones to care for who may feel as burdened and as stressed as I did. I want them to know that even if they can't see or hear anything, there are angels all around them.

Alfred was six when he saw an angel. Here's his story.

An open book

I remember the day I saw an angel crystal-clear. I am sure within my heart and soul that I did not imagine it and over the years it has been a source of great strength. I think it could have saved my life.

My uncle started to abuse me when I was four or five years old. I can't remember the exact time. All I know is that I don't have a memory of my childhood that didn't involve pain, confusion and guilt. Pain because his beatings and attacks hurt so bad; confusion because I didn't know why I was being touched, and guilt because I thought I was to blame.

The day I saw my angel I was outside our front door looking after my baby sister. She was so beautiful and I loved her beyond words. Even though I was only six, I wanted to take care of her. It was a really lovely day and I was enjoying the closeness between me and my sister. I wanted only good things for her. I prayed for good things for her. I didn't want her to suffer as I did. While I was thinking about my sister, I looked up at the sky and saw an angel that was the size of Big Ben. It seemed to glow like a light bulb of diamonds, although more beautiful and bright than that. It was dressed in a huge white robe that covered its feet and I could see enormous purple wings rising from its

111

back. There was a book in its hand and glowing light came from that book. I don't know if it was male or female as I could not see its face because of the brightness of the light. I was not imagining it. I saw an angel that day. I saw it for several minutes before it disappeared.

The abuse didn't stop after my angel vision but just thinking about it eased the pain. It helped me realise that there was someone or something out there who loved and cared for me. Also, seeing the angel read a book made a great impression on me and from that day on I got a passion for reading and schoolwork. The more I was beaten, the harder I would work.

When I was ten my teacher told Mum that I was a gifted student and I think it surprised her a lot, because she had always struggled at school and assumed I would. She treated me differently after that and stopped leaving me at home on my own with my sister so much. When my uncle came round to 'baby-sit', I told her that he made it hard for me to study so she stopped asking him round.

There's still more to tell. When I was eleven and my little sister was five, my uncle started to concentrate his attentions on her. I could recognise all the signs and I knew I had to stop it. I finally plucked up the courage to tell my mum and she was physically sick when I told her. She believed me and the last memory I have of my uncle is my mum shouting and throwing the phone book at him with such force that he almost passed out.

I'm in my fifty-fifth year now and I still think about my angel reading in the sky. I've been through years of counselling to help me come to terms with what happened to me as a child and I don't think I ever will completely, but that angel vision has remained a constant source of hope, comfort and inspiration. Please share my story because I hope

it will help other victims of abuse, be that abuse emotional or physical. I hope it will help them see that there can be light at the end of the
tunnel and that even if you can't see your guardian angel, he or she
exists.

Alfred's story is a painful reminder that bad things happen to
innocent people, but it is also a reminder that during times of
crisis and distress this life on earth is not all that there is. There
is an invisible world of hope, light, peace and love and it is from
this world that we are born and it is to this world that we will
eventually return when the time comes for us to cross over. It is
a reminder that we are spirit in a body, and while we are on earth
heaven hasn't disappeared. If we open our hearts it is very much
alive around and within us. All we need to do is believe.

With all the alarming and distressing news we are bombarded
with every day via newspapers, TV and online, heaven feels like
the right place to ponder and concentrate our thoughts and feelings on. We can all see angels if we cultivate an attitude of peace
and hope that ignites feelings of courage, power and trust in both
others and ourselves. And recognising that sometimes we can't do
anything except pray for help and guidance is a good place to
start.

Many times I'm asked what prayer is, and it is a word I don't
really like using because it is so strongly associated with religion –
and angels are non-denominational – but for those uncomfortable with the concept, prayer is simply a way of talking to your
angels. Intense, concentrated and heartfelt thoughts and feelings
are a form of prayer. As you've seen, your angels are always tuning

113

in to what goes on in your mind and in your heart, and therefore in spirit your thoughts and your feelings have great power.

Listening to your heart and believing in angels won't make everything in your life perfect or take away all your worries. What it can do, though, is help you see that however vulnerable, alone and in crisis you feel there is always a part of you – the eternal spirit in you – that can rise above anything that life throws at you, however painful or tough. And when you can rediscover that eternal spirit within you, when feelings of hope and love cluster in your heart, there is only ever light in your darkness and sweet music in your soul.

I'm aware that I've digressed here, so to return to the theme of this section – how people can feel and see their angels – I want to stress once again that visions and apparitions of angels are extremely unusual. Sure, there are people who can see angels outside of their mind, and in some cases it is possible to learn how to do this, but it is far more common for visions of angels to appear in our mind's eye or in our dreams. Seeing angels doesn't just refer to visions that appear outside of a person's head, but also to visions that appear *inside* your mind. Just because an image flashes through your mind does not make it any the less valid, real or life-changing, as these next three stories show. We'll start with Mona. I've transcribed her incredible story for you from a phone conversation:

Starlight

I was born completely blind. I'm still blind today and experience the world through touch, smell and hearing, but in my dreams and my daydreams I can see angels. It started when I was about four years old and hasn't stopped. I'm forty-four now and I still see them. When I was about five, I started to draw my angels. My mum and dad and my doctor were amazed. They told me the figures I was drawing had wings and flowing robes and they don't know how I could know what angels looked like because they had never talked about them with me. I told them that I knew because I could see angels inside my head. And when I see them they have a starlight glow around them, a glow that I know can't be seen on earth.

I used to think I was imagining my angels but over the years I have come to understand that the angels in my mind and my dreams have their own very real presence. They are my lights in the darkness. They illuminate my world. I feel truly blessed that I am able to see them and feel sorry for the normal-sighted who can't because I know if they saw what I see every day – the rainbow of beauty, light and colour and the starlight glow of love – they would feel as at peace with themselves and the world around them as I am. They would know that wherever we go and whatever we do, there are angels around and inside us, guiding and loving us.

I've never met Mona but I have spoken to her and her voice is as gentle as her words. Indeed, while I was speaking to her I glanced at the wall and saw sparkling dots of light dancing there – a confirmation to me that she is right, angels do indeed surround us.

Like Mona, Patricia also believes she 'sees' angels.

Nine to five

I believe in angels because I have seen one in my office, of all places. It happened last year when I was working late. Most of my colleagues had gone home but I felt I needed to put in the extra time. I had told my secretary to go home but she insisted on staying to help me out.

It must have been about eight pm when I felt my eyes getting tired so I thought I would close them for a few minutes to recharge. When I did I had the most astonishing experience. I saw a tall beautiful man. He didn't scare me because he looked so beautiful and calm. I could see huge glowing wings behind him and he looked over ten feet tall. He held out his hand and told me that sometimes I needed to work to live. I immediately felt all stress and tension go out of my body. It was like stepping into a warm bath at the end of a busy day. I was scared to open my eyes because I didn't want him to disappear, so I kept them closed for as long as I could.

So there I was just sitting there with my eyes closed when I felt my secretary gently tapping my arm and heard her asking me if I was all right. Startled, I opened my eyes and she told me that as devoted as she was to her job it was time for her go home now. She kept on apologising because she felt she was letting me down. I told her that couldn't be further from the truth and then she said something that took my breath away. She told me that she admired me because my job was my passion, but for her it was just work and that was the difference between us two – I lived to work and she worked to live.

I will never forget what my secretary said that night and how it echoed the words of my angel. My husband has tried to tell me I must have fallen asleep and it was just a coincidence but I know I did not fall asleep. I was sitting upright for a start, and that's how my secretary found me. I feel in my heart that my experience was real. There was an angel in my office that night, gently reminding me that there is more to life than work. I have heeded the message, and although I still have workaholic tendencies I make sure they never take over my life again.

Jack is convinced that he doesn't imagine the angels he 'sees'.

The edge of reason

I often see angels. It typically happens when I am just about to fall asleep or wake up or when I am in a particularly long and boring meeting at work. I also see them when I go on train journeys or any time really when I let my mind go blank, and empty it of thoughts and worries. I see them both with my eyes closed and with them open. It usually starts with a smiling angel face. I always smile back and the angel smiles again and then more angels appear. They all have such gentle, beautiful faces. Sometimes I see their wings and gowns, and sometimes it's just the faces. There is one angel in particular I see a lot. Hope this doesn't sound odd, but it looks a bit like me, or a happier, wiser, calmer version of me. Do you think he could be my guardian angel? There are no words in my vision, just smiling angels and bright lights. It's gorgeous. Then I will hear a rushing noise and they disappear in a flash.

I only told my brother about my angel visions and wish I hadn't because he just laughed and told me I was a nutjob. I didn't think I would tell anyone else about it because of how he reacted but then I came across your book and read a story about a guy who had similar experiences when he was just about to fall asleep. It was very comforting to have it confirmed that I'm not losing it, but if I think about it, deep down I knew that all along. The angels I see are not hallucinations and

I'm not going nuts. I am perfectly sane and rational and have a very responsible job as a dentist. In fact, I have come to the conclusion that when I daydream I have the ability to enter a kind of altered state where aspects of the invisible psychic world become visible to me. I see what is around us all the time, just not visible.

Jack makes an interesting and valid point here. Even the most sceptical of people know that this earthly life is not all that there is. There is another level of reality, another dimension, an invisible spiritual dimension. Anyone who has trouble accepting this idea might want to think about radio waves. We know the waves are there, even though we can't see, feel or touch them. Like radio waves an invisible spiritual dimension also exists and when you tune into that dimension you may be able to hear your angels speaking. Angels are messengers from that dimension. Remember, the true meaning of the word angel is 'messenger'.

When people ask me why they haven't seen their guardian angel and I explain to them that mental images of angels can be just as real and valid as external ones, they often tell me that they have been seeing angels all along, they just didn't realise it until now. It's a wonderful 'ah-ha' moment for them. If you don't think you have seen or heard angels I hope it will be a moment of inspiration for you too. I hope it will help you understand that for the great majority of us, myself included, angel encounters aren't about dramatic, out-of-this-world external encounters but about subtle, gentle, silent, internal realisations that open our minds and our hearts to the invisible world.

So, if the only way you can see angels is to imagine, dream or daydream about them or to look up in the sky and notice an angel-shaped cloud or to recognise their presence in a feather or in animals, insects and the natural world, then you are still encountering angels. We talk more about angel signs or calling cards, as well as night visions and dreaming, in chapters six and seven, but for now whether your encounters appear in your mind's eye, in your heart or are external is irrelevant. What matters is that you notice and give attention to these images, because they are all visual messages from heaven.

Light years ahead

Before I stop talking about different ways to see angels, I want to touch on a subject that in recent years has increasingly come to my attention as a way for angels to show themselves to us, and that is as orbs of light. These light orbs most typically appear in photographs, but sometimes, as was the case for Nancy who tells her story below, they can flash right in front of our eyes.

Light eyes

Towards the end of 2005 I started to see flickers of bright light every night before I fell asleep. The only thing I can compare it to is when you look at something bright, like a light bulb or candle, for too long and then when you close your eyes you see flashing images. For me, though, I was seeing all this with my eyes open and I had not been staring at anything bright before I went to sleep. The bright lights didn't frighten me at all. They felt warm and loving and after a while I got used to them. Before long I began to see small figures in the centre of the lights and then after that I could see their tiny faces. It was awesome.

This went on for about three months and then I was diagnosed with ovarian cancer, fourth stage, in March 2006. My treatment programme began immediately and I was told that my chances were not good. It was a hellish time, emotionally and physically, and my only source of comfort, apart from the love of my family, was my bright shining lights. They gave me such solace and I really thought they were preparing me for my final journey, but five weeks into my therapy I fell asleep for the first time without seeing my bright lights. I was devastated. I really missed them. I didn't see them for about four weeks and then everything fell into place when my doctor gave me the all-clear. He told me my recovery was astonishing. My treatment had been effective and my tumours were disappearing.

For the past few years I have been cancer-free and I have not seen my bright lights again.

I have received a number of emails and letters from people like Nancy who have seen orbs with their naked eyes. From what I have been told the experience is similar to the way that all of us see a bolt of lightning. As lightning strikes there is a flash of bright intense light that lasts for a matter of seconds. However, as mentioned above, seeing orbs with your naked eye is less common than orbs appearing in photographs.

Today, orbs are a genuine light phenomenon that is being observed and photographed around the world and even in outer space. These transparent orbs were first captured by film cameras when a flash was used. However, recently, digital flash cameras have been recording the same strange spheres of light. It's always a lovely moment when one of my readers writes to me and sends an orb photograph by post or via email. Often the image manifests as a small orb or globe of light when the photo is developed. These orbs present in a multitude of colours including white, yellow, orange, pink, red, green, blue, purple and in combination, like a rainbow.

Typically invisible to the human eye, these orbs suddenly and inexplicably appear on a photograph, most typically over babies and children, but also over adults who are spiritually minded. In some photographs it is even possible to recognise faces appearing in the orbs. I find this truly incredible. I don't know if these faces are of angels or the faces of departed loved ones, but in my opinion the majority are best described as higher forms of spiritual beings, such as angels and archangels. Like us, spirit beings are all unique and individual and their energy status and roles vary in the big picture. If you still aren't sure what I'm talking about, just type in the words 'angel orbs' on the internet and you'll find thousands upon thousands of engrossing images.

Frequently when people send me pictures of orbs they ask me if they should get them tested to make absolutely sure they are seeing angels. As far as testing is concerned I have done my own research over the years. I have discussed the phenomenon of orbs with a number of parapsychologists and professional photographers, and a significant number have told me that orb photographs, from all kinds of cameras – film and digital – don't always match the commonly recognised image reflection patterns of dust, pollen, moisture or camera lens light flares. In other words, they don't know what is causing them to appear.

If you do come across an orb in a photograph you could send it for testing and analysis as I have done, but in many ways it doesn't really matter what the end result of that analysis is. What matters, in my view, are the feelings that seeing orbs inspire in you. When you gaze at photographs of orbs, if they make you feel inspired and excited, in my mind their origin is angelic. If you open your heart and mind to their presence, and allow yourself to feel the images, they can be a reminder that there is more to see in this world than your mind can comprehend.

I didn't really know much about photographic orbs until people started to send them in to me. I had a vague idea that they were associated with the paranormal in some way but I never really gave them much thought. Now, however, I am absolutely convinced that they offer physical proof of angels adapting themselves to the twenty-first century by lowering their spiritual frequency or energy to express their being in orbs that radiate light, love and healing.

Can you ever be really sure?

You'll have seen by now that angels can appear in many different ways, and that is part of their magic and wonder. In the previous chapter we talked about distinguishing between the voice of your angel and the voice of fear or wishful thinking, and as we close this chapter I find myself returning to the same theme. With so many different manifestations and their awesome ability to reach out to us through our feelings and through images and dreams, both inside and outside our minds, how can you ever really be sure that it is angels talking to you?

You can be sure because whenever you are inspired to change from one way of living or thinking or feeling to a more positive, uplifting way of living or thinking or feeling, your angels are speaking to you, loud and clear. You had help. If you aren't sure or don't understand the messages being sent to you, your guardian angel will try to find another way to communicate, until you do understand. And the angels will never give up on you. They will continue trying different ways until they find one that grabs your attention.

In other words, angels will keep trying to speak to you, things will keep happening until you do understand. Angels will keep calling out to you, sending you their messages from heaven, until you understand that you are not a human being having a spiritual experience, but a spiritual being having a human experience. And, as the next chapter shows, nothing can give this eternal truth more clarity than messages sent from beyond the grave.

CHAPTER 5

Talking to the Other Side

> *Of course you don't die. Nobody dies. Death*
> *doesn't exist. You only reach a new level of vision,*
> *a new realm of consciousness, a new unknown*
> *world.*
>
> Henry Miller

I don't know exactly what happens to us after we die. Some people believe that this earth is all there is, the only reality, and once we breathe our last we are gone for ever. Others believe in reincarnation – the idea that when we die our spirits return many times to learn new spiritual lessons. Others believe in the concept of reward and punishment in the afterlife. And then there are those, and I count myself among them, who are absolutely convinced that when we die our spirits survive the death of our bodies and continue to live in another realm or level of existence that we simply cannot understand while we are in human form.

You may wonder how I can be so sure. I'm sure because of the countless numbers of stories about contact with the afterlife that

I have come across in the twenty-five years I have been researching and writing about the psychic world. I'm sure because I grew
up in a family of psychics and spiritualists and although I am not
a psychic or a medium myself I have witnessed and experienced
some extraordinary things. For instance, I believe I have been visited by both my departed parents in my dreams, and the messages
they have communicated to me have been both life-saving and
life-transforming. And finally, I'm also sure because I believe that
the existence of an afterlife is, contrary to popular belief, perfectly
logical.

Think about it. Modern science tells us that everything – this
book, you, me, your house, your mobile, your teacup – consists
of energy. Every part of the universe is nothing more than pul-
sating units of energy and the way in which it pulsates determines
how it manifests on earth. Your body, your thoughts, your feelings are all energy. Is it so ridiculous to believe then that when
our body dies, the energy that has given us life, the energy that
has inspired our minds and hearts, continues to exist? Could this
energy not live in another realm of existence? And could this
energy still interact with the living?

Since the beginnings of recorded time there have been
accounts of people who believe they have been visited in some
way by their loved ones after death. Is it the force of the energy
between those who love or share strong bonds with each other
that makes communication with the afterlife possible? In this
chapter you'll see that afterlife communication isn't just possible,
it really happens and it happens to ordinary people every day.

There are many ways that the spirits of departed loved ones

can communicate with us, and I'll try to review as many as possible here. First of all, though, I do need to clarify how angels are related to the spirits of those who have died. As I always stress in my books, it seems unlikely that our loved ones become angels. Although we often like to think of a departed loved one becoming an angel, angels are a different kind of entity to the spirits of the departed because they are pure beings of spirit that have never lived on earth. Despite this, the overwhelming majority of accounts of visitations from beyond the grave share strong similarities with accounts of visitations from angels, most typically a life-transforming sense of peace, love and comfort. This has led me to believe that spirits of departed loved ones can be guided back to loved ones on earth through the intervention of an angel. Therefore in this book, and indeed all my books, I like to use the word 'angel' and the word 'spirit' interchangeably because the message of hope, love and comfort they bring from the other side is one and the same.

To return to the different ways our loved ones in spirit can talk to us, I'm going to begin with one of the most common ways and that is through our dreams. This is Rachel's story.

Afraid of the dark

I've always been very scared of the dark. From an early age I could only be left in my room if there was a light on. It drove my mum mad. She worried like crazy about me. I've got better over the years but even now, at the age of thirty-five, I'm still very jumpy. I believe in an afterlife but the idea of ghosts and spirits really scares me; freaks me out really, if I'm honest. That's why I can't believe I am sending you this story about my dad, and what happened to me doesn't feel frightening at all. Just the opposite in fact: it's given me an enormous amount of courage and hope.

Three years ago my dad died. I wasn't there with him when he died and it tore me apart. I was on holiday in Australia with my husband and three kids and we just couldn't get a flight back in time. I knew he was ill when we left – he had cancer – but there wasn't any indication that he was so close to passing. Doctors had told us that he had at least six months. How wrong they were! I only just got back in time for the funeral.

A week after the funeral the dreams started. I began to have recurring dreams of my dad sitting on the end of my bed reading to me. He was reading this book called *The First Five People You Meet in Heaven*. The stunning thing was that it felt so real, not like a dream at all. I would wake up and still hear his voice lingering in my mind. At first the dreams unsettled me quite a bit because I would often wake up convinced that my father was in my bedroom. I wondered if I was losing it. Was it possible that my father had been in my room? On one occasion I even saw an indent on the bed in the exact same spot he had been sitting in my dream.

I told myself it had to be a dream, nothing but a dream. Also, it didn't add up. My father had not been an educated man and the only thing I had ever seen him read was the football results. He didn't do books. The experience was so compelling, though, that I decided to talk to my sister about it and when I told her she gave me the strangest look. She told me that in the week before Dad's death she had spent a lot of time with him in hospital and when it was obvious that the end was close she rarely left the hospital. It was then that she had got in touch with me to tell me the sad news, but I had had problems getting a flight back.

Anyway, during those few days prior to my dad's death she came across a copy of *The First Five People You Meet in Heaven* in the hospital canteen. It didn't seem to belong to anyone and the title intrigued her and she started to read it and had been instantly engrossed.

My sister never told me about this book and I had never heard of it before. I just couldn't explain how I saw my father reading it. The dreams stopped as soon as I told my sister about them and not surprisingly I found myself drawn to the book. My father had been reading it to me, so surely there had to be some message for me. I found out that it is by an author called Mitch Albom and it tells the story of a simple but dignified old man, Eddie. After dying in a freak accident, Eddie finds himself in heaven where he encounters five people who have significantly affected his life, whether he realised at the time or not. I also found out that the author wanted it to be read by people who felt they were unimportant here on earth so that they would realise, finally, how much they mattered and how much they were loved.

I had always known my father loved me but there were times when his busy media career did make me feel like I didn't matter very much. I don't have any memories of him when I was a young child because he travelled a lot. It was always just me, Mum and my sister, and my mum was always worried about burglars or intruders without Dad around, so perhaps that's where my fear of the dark came from. Looking back I had always longed for his attention and approval but never really got it. I also felt that because I got married fairly young and never had a career like my sister I was a disappointment to him.

I don't think that any more, just as I'm not afraid of the dark any more. I really believe my dad talked to me in my dreams and I feel that he is watching over me and loving me wherever he is.

It really does seem that in death Rachel's father wanted to let her know that even though he didn't show it as much as he could have done on earth, he loved her very much and she mattered greatly to him. And her dreams became the medium he chose to express this love and reassurance. This next dream is also one that concerns the love of a father and his daughter. It was sent to me by Ellie.

A dozen red roses

It was two summers ago. I was tired and it was the middle of the day, around three pm, so I decided to lie down on the couch and take a short nap. Like always, and until this day, I had several dreams while sleeping. The last dream I had was just before I woke up. I knew that because it actually woke me up.

I dreamt that my father was sitting with my boyfriend and they were driving on a two-lane highway to come and see me. It was dark and my boyfriend went to pass another car but hit a white truck head on and died. In my dream I saw his dead body and there were red roses scattered all over it. It was a horrible scene, but it didn't scare me because my father was standing close by and he told me everything was going to be OK.

I woke with a start and with a lot on my mind. First of all, my father died five years ago, and this was the first time he had appeared so vividly in my dreams. As for my boyfriend, he was very much alive. I also knew that he had to take a two-lane highway to come and see me because he lived an hour's drive away. So, panicking because of my dream, I immediately called him at work. When he answered I told him that I was concerned about him driving to see me today, because I had had a dream that he might crash. I didn't tell him any details about the dream, or that my father had been in it too, just that I had seen him get killed. He just laughed and told me not to worry.

I tried hard to stop him but that night he did come and see me. When he arrived at my house he looked stressed but had a smile on his face and a dozen red roses in his hands. (I also hadn't told him about the roses I had seen in my dream, and he'd never been one to buy me flowers before.) He came in and sat down and told me he had tried to change lanes and had almost been hit head-on by a white truck. He said if I hadn't told him about the dream I'd had, he wouldn't have been aware of his driving that night. He admitted to me that despite initially dismissing it when I called him, my dream warning had affected him. He believes, as I do, that my dream saved his life. I also believe that my father was somehow warning me. Do you think that might be possible?

I emailed Ellie back to say I didn't just think it was possible, I was in no doubt that it was possible. Although specific messages and warnings that come at exactly the right time from loved ones in spirit are rare, I have read enough of them by now to know that they do occur. I also have personal experience of them myself. It could be said that instances like this are more about intuition, but as you've seen, angels can also speak to us through our intuition.

And whether heaven talks to us through our dreams, or via our intuition, the effect is equally wondrous. This is how it felt for Laura.

Big Mama

On 1 January 2009, our beloved great-grandma (Big Mama) sadly passed away due to heart/chest problems. A few months before Christmas Big Mama had become very ill, but at least she got one last wish and spent Christmas at home, rather than in hospital.

A week before her funeral I had this dream/vision in which I and my little younger brother Ryan were standing at a roadside near a lovely little park. I remember the weather in this dream/vision: it was warm and sunny (I could actually feel the sunshine). Then all of sudden from nowhere our great-grandmother appeared, she was 'hovering' and she did not speak, she just smiled and waved! She looked twenty years younger and was glowing with health, just as I remember her when I was a little girl.

There was a small garden in the park in which three little girls where planting flowers. This seemed very appropriate as it really represented my great-grandma's spirit because during her 'earth life' she loved gardening and adored children. Ryan turned round to me and said, 'Big Mama, it was really her, did you see her?' I said, 'Yes, I did,' and then she was gone.

I woke up and for about a minute I forgot she had passed on but then when I woke up properly I realised. I remembered my beautiful dream. I had tears running down my face. I knew it was her way of letting us know she was OK.

A week or so later I told my dad about this dream and he said, 'It could mean you're going to have a baby in the near future and Big Mama wanted to tell you.' I said I didn't know about that! Would you believe it, I and my husband-to-be now have a beautiful four-month-old baby girl. Whatever the reason(s) for this lovely visit I know it helped me to realise that wherever Big Mama is, she is happy and well.

The bond of love created by family members for one another is an incredibly powerful force that can bring tremendous joy and help overcome problems and setbacks in life. And, as we see in this next story, sent to me by Simon, it can also cross the barrier between life and death to express itself in our dreams.

Good night

When my wife died five years ago I was left to raise my son and daughter alone. Mercifully, they were both over the age of ten so this made it easier for them in some ways, but not in others. Perhaps if they had been younger they may not have been so aware of their loss. I guess there is no right time for any child to lose a loving mother. There's also no right time for a husband to lose a wonderful wife. She died of breast cancer and I was with her to the end. I would have had it no other way. She was my life and I would have given mine to save hers, but it was not meant to be.

In the first few months I coped just about. Family and friends gathered around, determined to make sure I was never alone for more than a few hours. My sister came to stay with me and then my cousin and then Mum and Dad. Everybody told me how strong I was being and I told them I was being strong for the children. I didn't give my kids much time to grieve and ponder their loss. I made it my mission to keep them busy. A few weeks after the funeral, we went on a rock climbing holiday and then when we came back I sold the house and we moved to a much smaller house with a bigger garden. I also bought them a puppy each and if you've ever had a puppy you'll know how busy they can keep you. We'd fall asleep at night exhausted.

I managed to hide my pain during the day, but it always came back to hit me like a hammer hitting a bruise in the few moments before I fell asleep. I knew this would be the toughest time for my kids too so I would sit in their room with them until they drifted off. Sometimes it would take them a long time to fall asleep. How I longed for my wife then. How I longed to hear her whisper gently, 'Good night and sweet dreams,' as she always used to do. When they finally got to sleep I would sit watching TV or do the housework until exhaustion took over.

Most nights I would fall asleep almost instantly but some nights the pain in my heart kept me awake. I would cry silently into my pillow, feeling very alone and in need of comfort. It was on one of those nights, about ten months after my wife's death, that I had this reassuring dream.

In my dream I saw my grandmother. She had passed away many, many years before. I was happy to see her but the person I really wanted to see was my wife and I know my grandmother sensed this because I felt myself being drawn towards the house we used to live in. Once inside I saw my wife. She was walking upstairs to the children's bedroom – they had single beds in one room. I followed her. She didn't seem to be aware of me. I saw my wife enter the bedroom and then sit down on my son's bed. I saw my son sleeping and I saw my wife bend down and kiss him and whisper, 'Sweet dreams.' Then I saw her go to my daughter and do the same. I couldn't tear my eyes away from my wife. She had always been beautiful, but now she looked stunning. She looked healthy and vibrant. I longed to touch her but as soon as I reached out towards her she vanished and I woke up.

The next morning my son came down to breakfast and told me he had had a dream about Mum. We rarely mentioned her so this was unusual and I felt uncomfortable, but something inside me urged me to listen. I asked him about his dream and he told me that he had had a dream about Mum tucking him into his old bed and kissing him good night.

I was dumbstruck for a few minutes. Was it possible that my son and I had had the same dream on the same night? I grabbed my son and hugged him and we both cried. When I finally pulled away I noticed my daughter standing beside us. We told her about our dreams and she then told us something even more astonishing. She had also dreamt of her mum. In her dream she had not been tucked into bed but had spent time chatting with Mum in the kitchen. She couldn't remember what they had chatted about. It didn't really matter, what mattered was the feeling of closeness my daughter experienced.

As I listened to my children talk at length for the first time about their mother and how she had visited them in their dreams, I felt I was being given a wonderful gift by my wife – a real miracle. Those dreams have convinced me that there is an afterlife, and that my wife's spirit is all around us. Today we talk about my wife, their mum, all the time and the more we talk about her the more alive she feels to us. It is such a comfort to know that she watches over us and wants us all to have sweet dreams of her.

Simon's story is overwhelming not just because it is a compelling vision of a departed loved one, but because it also involves the phenomenon of a shared dream. It seems that Simon and his children experienced the very same dream on the very same night. Shared dreaming is rare, but it does occur and I have had several stories sent to me about people who are close in some way, having similar or identical dreams on the same night. There could, of course, be an empathetic influence at work. For example, in Simon's case his children may simply have tuned into their grieving father's feelings and vice versa, but as you know it is my belief that in our dreams the living can mingle with the dead and we can meet those who have passed over.

Indeed, one of the easiest ways to connect with a loved one in spirit is through our dreams, because when we are asleep our subconscious is more open and receptive to receiving messages from the other side. Dreams are also one of the safest and gentlest ways for loved ones to make contact without causing distress or alarm. In the months and years following my mother's death I longed for some reassurance from her that she hadn't gone far away, and the medium she chose to reach out to me first was through my dreams. It was by far and away the best choice for me because at the time I just wasn't ready for anything else. I had too much fear and self-doubt and these would have closed my mind, my heart and my eyes to anything else.

Without doubt, dreams of the departed are emotionally compelling. I have received countless stories from people who have had dreams of loved ones in spirit and all are convinced that the experience was real in a spiritual way. They all believe they were visited by the dead and that they received a message of comfort and reassurance. Such dreams are more likely to occur on anniversaries and birthdays. As Sylvia's story shows, it is as if loved ones in spirit want to share these special days with us.

Everywhere

My mum always had health problems, high blood pressure and a heart condition. She was always talking about it, worrying about it, but you always think of your parents as immortal. When I came home from work one day Mum's health was the last thing on my mind, but then I was told she had had a stroke.

For the next three weeks we still had hope but then she aspirated and it was all over. I would never see her again. We decided to cremate her. Mum always loved the sea so we took her ashes on a boat and scattered them at sea. I have often been asked if I miss having a gravesite to visit, some plot of land where I can sit quietly and talk to her. At the very least shouldn't I go out on a boat and visit the area of shore where we scattered her ashes?

At first I did miss having somewhere to go and it was especially hard on my first birthday after her death. Mum and I had always had this lovely ritual on my special day. Nothing special, we just went shopping and had coffee, but it was our special time together. When I fell asleep the night before my birthday I dreaded waking up without Mum being there and it was on that night that I had my first dream about her since she died. In my dream we went shopping and had coffee and then just before I woke up I heard her say to me that she was everywhere I was.

It's been nearly two and a half years since Mum died and I dream of her lots of times. The dreams feel so real and so vivid that sometimes I wake up and can't believe she has gone. So when people ask me if I miss visiting a gravesite, I tell them that I do not. I tell them that she is everywhere I am. As I am writing to you now, although I am many miles and years from where my mother's ashes were scattered, she is with me. She is the air that I breathe and the breeze that lifts my hair. I feel her in my laughter and in my tears. I felt her when my son was born and she is with me whenever I visit Dad, who is suffering from Alzheimer's. I speak to her in my home, in my car and in the distance between the earth and the stars. I also visit her in my dreams – for they bring me as close to heaven as I may ever know. I used to think there was no comfort in losing someone you love, but now I understand that there can be comfort and I can find that comfort everywhere I am.

Please share my story with others as I hope it will help those grieving the loss of a loved one to move forward. I'd also like to send you this poem, which always inspires and comforts me.

> Death is nothing at all.
> I have only slipped away to the next room.
> I am I and you are you.
> Whatever we were to each other,
> That, we still are.
> Call me by my old familiar name.
> Speak to me in the easy way
> which you always used.
> Put no difference into your tone.

Wear no forced air of solemnity or sorrow.

Laugh as we always laughed
at the little jokes we enjoyed together.
Play, smile, think of me. Pray for me.
Let my name be ever the household word
that it always was.
Let it be spoken without effect.
Without the trace of a shadow on it.

Life means all that it ever meant.
It is the same that it ever was.
There is absolute unbroken continuity.
Why should I be out of mind
because I am out of sight?

I am but waiting for you.
For an interval.
Somewhere. Very near.
Just around the corner.
All is well.

Henry Scott Holland

Deceased loved ones can also visit us in our dreams to offer guidance and support during times of trauma and crisis. This is Lucy's compelling story.

Turning point

My father took his own life when I was seventeen. I came home and found him. I stopped my little sister coming in and called an ambulance. When they arrived he was pronounced dead. He had taken an overdose. My mum had died the year before and I don't think he felt life was worth living without her. I went to live with my aunt and uncle. I felt so alone. I used to be very close to my dad. I thought he loved me. The hardest part was going to sleep at night. I would close my eyes and picture my father's dead body the way I'd found it. I missed him so much but I also hated him for deserting me, for giving up on me.

I hated living with my aunt and uncle. It wasn't their fault. It was mine. I think I would have hated living with anyone, because I hated myself. I hated not being enough for my father to live for. I left home and lived on the streets for six months. I sold my body for food and my soul for drugs. I was a mess, a desperate mess, until the night I had a dream about my father.

This dream was impossible to forget. It happened on 17 November 1998. I was sleeping outside a department store and I was tired, hungry and disgusted with life. In my dream I saw my father. It was the strangest thing. He was sleeping rough outside a department store, just like me. I watched him sleep and heard him say in his sleep, 'Help me, please, help me.' I asked him how I could help and he said, 'Take care of me, and then I can be with your mother.' I told him that I would and I held out my hand to him. When he took it I woke up. I felt this bubble of energy and happiness in me. I just knew that through my dream my father was telling me to turn my life around. He had died to be with Mum, but in my dream he was choosing instead to stay beside me. He still loved me and despite everything I still loved my father and I didn't want him to suffer any more.

I went home that day and started to build bridges with my family. I still don't know why my father did what he did and a part of me will always be angry with him for it, but twelve years on I have come to terms with it and that compelling dream was the turning point. I could be mad to think this but I believe my father knew he had let me down and sensed my grief and anger. It trapped him, just as his suicide trapped me. He couldn't move on in spirit to be with Mum until I moved on and started taking care of myself.

Suicide is such an emotive subject and I am deeply grateful for Lucy's courage in sending me her story. I don't have all the answers, but I do know that the reason for our existence is to learn to love. It sounds simple but love is not easy. Love has so many different aspects. One of the most basic and hardest lessons we need to learn is love of self, because until we learn that we cannot know how to love others. In Lucy's story, her father hadn't been able to master unconditional love of self and this had led him on a path of self-destruction that didn't end with his death and threatened to engulf his daughter too. In the afterlife he lived and breathed his daughter's pain. There was no escape. Both father and daughter needed to learn that in both this life and the next, self-love was the first and most important step, and that is why he sent her such a powerful dream message.

Many doctors and psychologists would argue that dreams of the departed are nothing more complex than creations of the grieving mind searching for any kind of comfort, even if it is temporary, in the hurt of losing someone you love. There is certainly a great deal of logic to this argument, but the more I read and hear about such dreams the more I believe they are indeed messages from beyond the grave.

First of all, if temporary pain relief was the only explanation, how come not everyone who has lost a loved one experiences such dreams? Secondly, many people who have such dreams say they are comforted by them or were able to move forward in their life afterwards. In my experience people who are grieving the loss of someone they love are often in a tight grip of pain, confusion, guilt, fear and anger. It is unusual for comforting and uplifting images to arise from these difficult emotions, making it all the more likely they come from a higher, spiritual source. Thirdly, what about dreams, like this one sent to me by Emma below, where the dreamer has no idea that someone has recently departed?

It's been fun

This is my true story. I don't understand how or why it happened and I am hoping you will enlighten me. I haven't had any such experiences before or since. Here goes.

I'm a university lecturer and each year I get a whole new intake of students in my tutor group. The groups are usually fairly small – about five or six – and they are usually very challenging and enjoyable. I get the odd difficult student but nothing I can't handle, until last year when I met Steven. It's not his real name but I shall use it here. Anyway, Steven seemed determined to challenge me on everything. He was exceptionally bright so I kind of enjoyed it, but I did worry that it might become wearing.

We were about two weeks into the first term when I had this really colourful and vibrant dream about him. In my dream I saw him walking up a large yellow and purple staircase. I called out to him and he turned to me and waved. I tried to wave back but my arms would not move. He laughed and said, 'It's been fun. I'm going now. Keep working them hard.'

I woke up but soon forgot about my dream as I had a busy day of lectures ahead. It wasn't until two pm that I heard the news. Steven had died. How do you explain that? I mean, I had only known him for two weeks!

Also hard to explain away are dreams that defy rational explanation, like this one sent to me by Anja.

Brown eyes

I dreamt that I was standing with my boyfriend Liam in my apartment with a baby girl in my arms. Liam was standing right behind me watching her over my right shoulder. We had made a bet – whose eyes she would have – and we waited for her to open her eyes to see the colour of them because we still didn't know in the dream. Finally she opened them and I was moved in the deepest of ways as her eyes were brown and looked exactly like mine.

I had this dream one year before Liam and I decided we wanted children and before I knew I could have children, because about a month after this dream, I was told by my doctor that due to polycystic ovaries

I might not be able to have children. So my little girl already knew better, visited me in my dream in advance to tell me that yes, she would come to us, yes, I could have a baby, and yes, she would be a girl with exactly the same brown eyes as mine.

Stories like this do suggest that in our dreams we can reach out to others through space and time, connecting with them before they are born and after they have died.

And to return to my arguments for dreams being messages from the world of spirit, there are a number of hallmarks of dreams of the recently departed that set them apart from other kinds of dreams with purely symbolic messages for you to interpret. One of the most noticeable is that spirit communication in a dream will feel very real and, unlike most dreams, when you wake up it will be impossible to forget. Again, unlike other dreams where the details are typically hazy, you will remember every detail vividly, and the images will linger in your mind for months and sometimes years after the dream. You are also unlikely to feel groggy when you wake up. In fact, you will feel energised. Also, there aren't usually other dream characters – just you and the departed. As pointed out previously, afterwards the dreamer feels overwhelmingly that the experience was real, the setting was realistic – for example the dreamer's bedroom – and they actually spoke to a loved one in spirit. Often the personality of the departed will be so recognisable that the dreamer is left in no doubt they came to visit them in their sleep. Many people who have had such dreams say they feel greatly comforted by them or can move forward from their pain and grief and sense of loss afterwards. Most typically the messages are reassuring: 'I'm fine. I love you and always will', and so on.

I'm often asked if there is a way to increase the chances of a loved one in spirit coming to you in a dream. Yes! Your dearly departed loved ones could just be a dream away. Just before you drift off to sleep it helps to focus on the deceased loved one you want to reach. Ask them to come to you in a dream and ask your angels to help guide them to you. This opens the way for loved ones in spirit to find you. Be patient – it may take many attempts and there is always a chance that a spirit will not come, not because they don't want to or don't love you, but because they need to progress with their spiritual development on the other side, or because they simply don't yet know how to enter your dreams. That's why asking your angels to help guide them is so crucial.

So, taking all the above into consideration, if you wake up one morning with memories of a vivid and realistic dream of a lost loved one, don't automatically assume it is just a normal part of the grieving process. It could well be that you have received a message from the afterlife. And don't get anxious if you haven't had such dreams yet. It took several long years after the death of my mother when I was busy raising a family before she finally graced my dreams. Just keep hoping that it will happen, and then one day when you least expect it, it will. As with many things in life, wanting deeply and then surrendering completely the want is what will finally make it happen.

I'd like to move away from dreams now to other ways that our departed loved ones can reach out to us. Harry didn't communicate at length with a loved one in spirit, but he believes he actually caught a glimpse of them on the other side. Here's his account.

Light of my life

Losing a child is the very definition of hell. My beautiful, lovely, bright daughter Megan died from AIDS after receiving a blood transfusion. Before she died I would have said I believed in something although I wasn't sure what, but after she died I believed in nothing. It had the opposite effect on my wife. She turned to spiritual healing for comfort. She would tell me that she felt Megan, our daughter, all around her. I couldn't feel anything. The only thing I could feel was emptiness. We hadn't been blessed with any other children, you see. She really had been the light of my life.

Eleven months after Megan died I was fast turning into an angry, bitter old man. I rarely went out and when I did I longed to be back in the comfort of my own home. I spent hours staring at photographs of Megan and hours cursing the misery and injustice of AIDS.

One evening as I was watching the news, out of the corner of my eye I saw something move. I glanced up and saw Megan standing in front of me. I rubbed my eyes, thinking I had finally lost it, but when I opened them she was still standing there. She looked radiantly happy. She didn't say or do anything; she just stood there. She was dressed in a pair of blue jeans and a rainbow-coloured top I didn't recognise. I could feel the love she had for me pouring into my heart.

Just then the door opened and my wife walked in. The moment was gone. My beautiful daughter vanished. My wife sat down beside me and asked me what the matter was because without realising it I had

145

knocked over a cup of tea and it was all over my trousers and the carpet. I told my wife what I had seen. I described what Megan was wearing and the feeling of love and wonder she had communicated to me. Tears came into my wife's eyes and she ran out of the room. I thought I had upset her but a minute later she came back and in her hand she was holding the rainbow-coloured top I had seen in my vision.

My wife told me that Megan had really wanted this top while out shopping one day with her, but it was too expensive so they had reluctantly decided not to buy it. After Megan's funeral my wife remembered the top and for reasons she did not understand decided to buy it. Somehow owning it made her feel closer to Megan. My wife never told me about buying the top because she thought I would not understand her reasons for doing so.

We may never know why AIDS, along with other horrendous diseases, like cancer, exist until we are in spirit ourselves and able to see the bigger picture of all our lives, but one thing I do know is that our spirits can and do grow when we are under stress. I also know that diseases, like trauma and crisis, can be an opportunity for incredible growth and enlightenment, forcing us all to learn lessons of tolerance, understanding and acceptance and bringing out elements of our personality we do not recognise as part of ourselves. So many people who have lost loved ones prematurely or witnessed their suffering, question their own spirituality, the meaning of their life, and it is through this questioning that many come to understand that when we pass over to the other side, the only thing that matters is the love we have in our hearts. And when love is the only judge, we are truly all the same. No one group or person is chosen above another.

What I relish most about the stories that are sent to me on a daily basis, stories like the one above sent by Harry, is that the people who send them do not typically claim to be psychics or mediums. Quite the opposite – many tell me they didn't think they had any special powers at all, or that they could see, hear or sense angels until they have their experience. Once again this proves to me that we are all born with latent psychic powers. Some people may have developed these powers more than others, and there may be certain techniques you can learn to put your mind in a more receptive state, but heaven isn't for a select few born with the 'gift' but for everyone – the only requirements are an open mind and an open heart.

Most people hear or sense their departed loved ones rather than actually see them. Olivia sent me a tape-recording of her story and the excitement in her voice as she described it was clearly evident. I've transcribed her recording for you below.

The voice of an angel

I was seven when I heard the voice of an angel and that angel was my mother. She had died giving birth to my sister when I was five and after that my life was brutal. My father did his best to raise us but he wasn't the caring, sharing type and I spent most of my time with his sister, my aunt. She started to molest me and the more my father left me and my sister with her the more brutal her attacks became. After one afternoon of abuse I remember lying on the floor crying hysterically when

I suddenly heard my mother's voice. I just heard her say, 'Listen to me now, little one. It is going to go away. I will not leave you. I love you.'

Then I felt her brush the hair away from my face and a warm sensation flowed through me, as if I was being wrapped in warm towels. Instantly I felt calm and I knew that what was happening to me was not my fault. The sensation started to fade and I cried again, wanting it to come back. I heard my mum say, 'Shush now, little one,' and I kept hearing it and feeling her gently rocking me until I fell asleep. When I woke up my grandfather called round to take me home to my dad. My face must have looked red and swollen from the crying and when he looked at me I could tell that he knew what was going on. He asked me to tell him what had happened and, frightened of my aunt, I told him it was nothing. At that moment my aunt came in. I must have jumped back in fear or something because my reaction was enough to convince my grandfather that his suspicions were correct.

After that night I never saw my aunt again. Charges were never brought against her and one day when I feel brave enough I may decide to confront her but right now I am not at that place. I have come to the belief that everything happens for a reason, even cruel and violent things, and as a result of my abuse I have the ability, as I think my grandfather did, just to know when someone is being abused or beaten around. I'm currently training to be a social worker and I hope one day to use my intuition to help other abused children.

I sincerely thanked Olivia for her deeply personal story as it cannot have been easy for her to send it to me. In it she describes how she not only heard the voice of her mother but also felt her mother's invisible arms rock her and invisible hands brush the hair from her cheek. There was also a warm sensation of comfort and love, a sensation many people have written to me about over the years. It's often hard to describe and I feel Stephanie, whose son Oliver was stillborn, describes it far better than I can:

Hot chocolate

It was when I was lying there feeling hopeless that I felt this tingling sensation at the back of my neck. The feeling grew until I felt this all over my back. I closed my eyes and felt warmth, peace and love. In my mind's eye I could see my mother standing there with Oliver in her arms. I knew he would be safe and well looked after with her. I then felt an angel wrap its wings around me. Sounds daft but I can only compare the feeling to that of drinking hot chocolate in front of a warm fire on a bitterly cold day. It was a great experience and very moving – I shall never forget it. Memories of it helped me pull through the darkest period of my life. Every time I felt low I drew strength from it because I know I'm not alone and that although it may have been Oliver's time to go, he is not alone either.

Loved ones in spirit may also choose to communicate with us through our sense of smell. When you are thinking about a lost loved one you may suddenly smell a fragrance you associated with them, such as a distinctive perfume or cigar smoke, even though no one is wearing that perfume at the time or smoking near you. Or perhaps the glorious but unexplained scent of flowers or the energising scent of vanilla lifts your spirit.

There could also be times when you may simply sense the presence of a loved one close by. You can't explain why because you can't see them or hear them, but you just sense, as Guy did in his brief account below, they are close by.

Sitting pretty

Ten years ago I lost my wife. She died from complications after a routine operation. It was so sudden I never got time to adjust. I was a wreck and was given counselling. None of it really helped. Family and friends were great, but what made the greatest difference was my sofa! I was sitting on it one day flicking channels when I got this strong feeling that Felicity – that was her name – was sitting beside me. I could just feel her. It was so real. It felt as if she was going to snatch the remote as she always used to when I started channel flicking. I looked around and my heart sank when I realised that she wasn't actually there. I might have dismissed it as wishful thinking, but then I looked down at the seat beside me and there was an indent as if someone had been sitting there!

In his story Guy mentions another fairly well reported phenomenon, and one that I have personal experience of, and that is noticing an unexplained indent on a sofa or chair or bed in the place where you sensed a departed loved one was sitting. To return to the sense of familiarity that a loved one is close by and somehow very much alive, I'm ready to share this next incredibly moving story sent to me by Hayley.

Keilan's story

Hi, my name is Hayley and I'm a mum of two beautiful boys, Logan who is two, and Keilan, who was born asleep on 4 March 2010. This is his story.

I found out I was expecting Keilan in August 2009. He was a much wanted baby brother for Logan. I had a relatively easy pregnancy and we involved Logan as much as we could to prepare him for the arrival of his brother. He was growing to be rather a large baby and was measuring four weeks in front!

On Sunday 28 February our world fell apart. Keilan had stopped kicking. I was thirty-two weeks and three days pregnant. It was very unusual for him as he was so active, very rarely asleep and always protested whenever his brother rested his head on my bump! We had assumed he was just having a sleepy day and had gone to bed on the Saturday as normal.

At 1.45 am I woke up suddenly, and after about five minutes I heard the most awful sound in my stomach. I decided to have a bath to see if I could rouse Keilan. I had no joy and at nine am Sunday morning we went to the hospital. I sat on a heartbeat monitor on the maternity ward listening to what we thought was Keilan's heartbeat. Thirty minutes later a doctor came in to see me. He felt my wrist and told me it was my heartbeat. At that point I think we knew deep down things had gone terribly wrong, but couldn't bring ourselves to say it. We had a bedside scan and no heartbeat was found. I was reassured he could still be OK, that these scans weren't very accurate. A radiologist from Doncaster Royal Infirmary was called to scan me, and at 12.10 pm I was taken down to ultrasound, where I remember saying to the doctor, 'He's gone.'

At 12.21 pm our worst fears were confirmed. Keilan had gone. We were walked back to maternity in shock and taken to a private room, where we were left to absorb what had been said. I just wanted to go home. My husband Dan sat with his arms around me while we both sobbed. The midwife and doctor came back in and told me I could go home, and that I should come back when I was ready to have Keilan.

We went back to my mum's house to get Logan. We tried to go home but couldn't face Keilan's newly decorated bedroom so went back to Mum's instead. I don't really remember what happened between finding out he was gone and going in to be induced, I just remember thinking that I had to give birth for Dan and Logan – I couldn't see my bump if I looked straight ahead but they could. I went back into the labour ward on Tuesday to be induced and was given a tablet and told to go home and wait – I waited forty-eight hours and still nothing. Thursday morning I went back to hospital knowing that this time I wouldn't be coming out pregnant, that my baby would be born.

I had made the decision not to see Keilan. I wanted to remember him as the active baby that kicked so hard he hurt me, the baby that never slept. The chaplain at the hospital came in to see us. While I was in labour, we planned his funeral. It felt so wrong to be planning to say goodbye before we even got a chance to say hello.

I gave birth to Keilan Daniel Draycott at 5.23 pm on Thursday 4 March 2010, exactly seven weeks to his due date. He weighed 4lb 13oz. After I gave birth, the midwife curled him around my back for a lovely little cuddle then wrapped him in a towel and placed him in a cot behind the curtain so his daddy could go and meet him. I still to this day believe the day of Keilan's birth was harder on Dan than for me. I was ready to give birth to him; Dan on the other hand had to watch me in all that pain knowing that our baby wouldn't be coming home with us. The nurses told me Keilan was the absolute double of his dad.

I still believe I made the right decision not seeing Keilan because I don't feel like I have lost him. I had him in me for thirty-two weeks feeling his every move and constantly cuddling him. I also needed to detach Keilan's birth from Logan's birth. Both boys were back to back so the labours were very similar. I had to detach from giving birth to Logan knowing I was taking him home and giving birth to Keilan knowing I couldn't, if you know what I mean. How could I cuddle him and kiss him and then leave him there? I couldn't do it.

Despite the trauma of it all, on the day of Keilan's birth I didn't feel sad. I felt the need to celebrate – after all, I'd still given birth to a perfect, beautiful little boy. This wasn't the day he died but the day he was born. The following two weeks were a blur, even the funeral was. All I remember is looking around and thinking how awful it must be for everyone else.

Not too long ago we got our answers. Keilan had a heart defect and his bowels weren't attached properly. He may have survived this if he had been born, he may have been okay. It was a blood clot in my cord that made him go to sleep. All I know is there is no way I would have wanted my baby to suffer; while he was in me he didn't feel pain because I didn't. I would feel this pain a million times if it meant my baby didn't.

All the way through this I haven't felt alone. I've had an amazing support network of family and friends and the unconditional support of my husband, who felt this just as much as I did. There was one special person though who got me where I am today – Cheryl, the amazing lady who shared her own special angel with me. She knew how I was feeling; she understood.

Even when you have amazing support it's still such a lonely experience because it is very different for everyone involved. Dan feels different to me; his grief is not any more or less, just different. It was the same with my mum, my dad and my siblings. So my thought was that I would try to set up a support group not just for mums but for the whole family: dads who can talk to each other, grandparents to share their experience, mums who can meet and share their angel babies. As I've learnt, it makes it a little easier knowing there is someone who knows how you feel. So, we got to work and we are starting our Sleeping Angels support group. It is run in Dinnington; I found that it seemed a central location for most of South Yorkshire and North Nottinghamshire. There is no support group in Doncaster, Sheffield, Worksop and Retford, and only one in Rotherham.

Our first meeting took place on Friday 2 July at two pm at The Middleton Institute, Barleycroft Lane, Dinnington, and every other Friday from then onwards. Everyone is welcome – even if you aren't ready to talk and just want to sit and have a cup of tea, just knowing someone is there makes such a difference, new angel mummies or older ones, and it's not a pain that goes away, you just learn to live alongside it. If you do decide to use my story please feel free to give my email address: Hayley@sleepingangels.org.uk so anyone who is interested in coming along can get in touch with me.

As I write to you it's now been four months since Keilan went to be an angel and we miss him every single day. We still feel him all around us though. His big brother talks to his baby in the sky. It's something we will live with for the rest of our lives and the night I heard that sound in my stomach I knew deep down that Keilan was waking me up to say goodbye. It's not goodbye though, it's a 'see you soon', because we will see him again one day, and although that seems a lifetime to us for him it will be just seconds.

Like many parents who have lost precious children, Hayley feels a deep sense of closeness with Keilan every moment of every day. He is always with her, alive in spirit.

Tanya also has a story of loss and healing to share.

My angels

In 2003 I gave birth to a little girl and in 2006 another one. I felt they were gifts from heaven. In 2008 I fell pregnant again. I went for my first scan and they told me I was only eight weeks along. I kept asking because my dates did not feel right but the nurse said she was sure and everything was OK. Then on Friday 7 September 2008, I was walking to get Rhiannon, my six year old, from school. It was raining heavily and I felt my tummy go over and a pain. It was like I had been stabbed in the tummy; all I wanted to do was get to the school and home again.

Once home I went to the toilet and that is when it hit me. I had a brown discharge but no blood. I hoped my feeling was wrong, that I had got it all in a muddle and everything was OK. I went on the internet and looked up my symptoms and the word 'miscarriage' kept flashing up so I called the hospital who told me if I was not feeling pain and not bleeding I should not worry. I should have twenty-four hours' bed rest. I kept asking if I had lost my baby and was it normal to bleed at this stage, thinking I was only just twelve weeks.

I could not sleep all night. I lay awake, scared to move and waiting for that flicker to say, 'Mum, I'm OK.' In the morning there was more discharge so I phoned back, hoping for a different nurse so perhaps I could have a scan to ease my mind. I just got the same advice – go to bed for twenty-four hours. By Saturday night I was even more beside myself so I called back and told them straight that I thought my baby had gone, even though I was not bleeding and had no pain. They still did not want to scan me until the end of the week and the reason they gave was that they did not have the staff to do it sooner.

I called again on Sunday morning and was finally given the go-ahead for a scan. At the hospital I was shown into a waiting room where I had to wait for what seemed like forever. I remember going into the scan and covering my ears and closing my eyes and crying. When I finally looked up, I saw the man who was doing the scan just look at the floor and it was obvious he had read my notes and possibly the number of times I had called. No words were needed.

I was taken into a side room to be alone with my partner Dave until a doctor called us. I remember thinking, This is all over now. I was given a blood test and sent home without any information on what to look out for. I didn't have any pains when I was at home and I was terrified I might lose my baby down the toilet, like some rubbish I didn't care about. I wanted to say goodbye and how much I had been looking forward to watching him or her grow up. So every time I went to the toilet, Dave would stand holding me close and making sure we did not lose our baby like that.

A week later I went back to the hospital for another blood test and scan. It felt so unreal having a scan because you expect to be told your baby is doing fine but when we stared at the screen the image resembled a snowstorm. The nurse was called out at one point and I could not help but read my notes, and this was the moment Dave and I found out we were having twins. Still in a state of shock I was told that I was booked in the next day for a D and C and I found some comfort in the fact that my ordeal would soon be over. I was longing to begin healing but instead my worst nightmare started. I was told to be there for seven-thirty am but wasn't seen until ten am. Even then I was just asked a few questions. I told them then that I was spiritual and wanted to bless my babies.

At twelve noon I was still waiting. Feeling exhausted and frantic I asked to go for a walk but was told that I couldn't in case I was called in. Eventually at around half past two a nurse came in and handed me a piece of paper. Until then I had not thought about signing my babies over, but that is how it felt. I was told to take my time and talk to Dave about our wishes. Dave just wanted to get it over with as quickly as possible so he could move on, but I felt different. I wanted to lay my babies to rest and know where they would be or even take them home.

The heading of the consent form make me feel sick. It read 'Disposal of tissue'. I still hadn't signed it when a nurse came in and asked for it. She had quite a cold and offhand manner and asked me why I hadn't signed it. I told her I didn't have a pen. I felt like a child being told off in front of the whole school by a teacher. She told me that I could have got a pen and then handed me one of her own. Then I signed my babies over and asked for a cremation with other babies lost in the same way. I was told when the service would be so I could go. Then finally at five pm I was called down. The last thing I remember before my operation is holding my belly and telling my babies how much I loved them.

The next thing I remember is being woken up and feeling very alone. I was rolled onto one side and there was a baby in recovery right next to me being cuddled by a nurse who told her, 'Mummy is coming.' Just knowing that my babies were wrapped in nothing more than a tissue and put to one side and not cared for or told that they were loved was unbearable. I was then wheeled into another ward and put in a side room. I was given a sandwich and a cup of water. I lay in that room heartbroken. I was so tired and just wanted to sleep, so I gave Dave the food and drink.

When a nurse came in she told me it was time to get dressed and go home. I wasn't given any information or comfort from the nursing staff. All I wanted was someone to put their arms around me and tell me I was not alone and my babies knew they were loved and wanted.

When I got home again it was me doing all the calls for information and a few weeks later I was given a date and time and place for the service. I went and ordered two white roses. Dave and I were the only ones at the service. It was just me and him and a tiny little coffin that looked like a shoebox. Thinking we had got to say, 'Sweet dreams', we were just saying our goodbyes when a lady come up to us and said she was sorry but our 'units' were not in there. There had been a misunderstanding. She asked me who told us about the service. I told her that the hospital had and she said she would contact them.

The lady went away and called the hospital and then came back and told me my babies were still in London and she was just awaiting details of when their service would be. I had not even been told they were being sent to London. Seeing my pain she told me she would take over from here and within a few days she had got my babies out of

London and organised a service. We were finally able to say our good-byes and lay our babies to rest in a children's garden.

On the day our babies were laid to rest the undertaker got out of the car and handed Dave the coffin, saying, 'Would you like to hold your babies?' On top of a tiny coffin that fitted in his hand were the words 'Babies of Tanya Pearson'. Now it hit me. I was saying goodbye and I had not met them. All I had was the memory of a tiny coffin. How could I be sure they were inside? I felt I had nothing and no one to talk to who would understand and it was at that moment that an idea popped into my head, like a gift from heaven. I decided to find a bear that I could have personalised with the words 'Fly free and high', because I wanted my babies to be free and not feel the pain I was feeling now and to be high because I did not want think of them in a shallow grave. The words felt true to my heart.

Feeling energised and inspired by the love of my angel babies, I found a company called Bears of Comfort and had my bear designed for me.

I found support from other angel mums on Facebook and when I told them about or showed them my bear I was shocked at how many of them wanted one too. The company told me that because it was my design only I could order it so I started to order them for other people and send them to them when they arrived. Knowing that my angel babies were with me every step of the way, I wanted to do more and give others what I had never had so I set up my page – www.bearsofcomfort.org.uk.

The bears I send out are to help bring comfort and healing to parents who have lost beloved children. I have sent out many bears of comfort, with angel baby names on them, some part funded and some

I have fully funded. I know they will comfort parents when they want a cuddle, to help them remember they are never alone and their babies live on inside their hearts. Currently I am working on setting up Bears of Comfort as a non-profit-making charity and in time I hope that I won't need to sell any bears and I can send them out for free.

I deliberately didn't edit down the harrowing elements in Tanya's heartbreaking story because it shows how in the depths of despair spiritual healing and growth is possible when we understand that in spirit there is no death, that those we love never really die as long as they are alive in our hearts. Even though Tanya feels she has no physical memories of her angel babies, her story shows they are with her, inspiring every moment of every day and communicating with her all the time.

The loss of a baby or child through stillbirth, miscarriage, cot death, abortion or for any reason under any circumstances is overwhelming and shattering. It is a damaged dream and a disturbing reality. Parents have to deal with the loss of their hopes for their future, and putting the pieces of their lives back together can be a painfully tough task. I do hope, though, that reading Hayley's and Tanya's stories will show you that it is not an experience to keep silent about or try to forget. You need to go through the grieving process before you can move forward to a new relationship with your angel babies in spirit. You see, each baby or child that dies is just a cloud away. It was their time to go, for whatever reason. Perhaps in spirit they chose to give up their life for their parent's spiritual growth, or perhaps they chose to be reborn in spirit so they can forever watch over their parents.

Of course, it's not just losing a child that can shatter lives – losing anyone you love is devastating and rebuilding your life afterwards can be traumatic at whatever age or stage of life you are. When my mother died I was in my mid-twenties but in spirit I was little more than a helpless child. I couldn't cope at all. I lost all sense of direction and purpose in life. It took a lot of time and growing up for me to understand that in death your relationship with a lost loved one can be reborn. You may not be able to see or touch them physically any more but you can experience them in new and wonderful ways. They can stay alive in your heart and in the belief that in spirit they can be with you more intensely than ever before.

Sadly, in our culture today there is such a great fear of death, but I have made it my life's work to show that death is not an end but a brilliant new beginning. It is just another stage in your existence. There is so much more in store for your loved ones in spirit and for you. Your loved ones continue their spiritual growth and development as do you. When you love someone you give away a part of yourself and that is a lovely thing as long as you don't lose yourself. And so when a loved one passes over, amid all the pain there is an opportunity for you to reclaim that part of yourself, the creative, loving power that is yours. Clearly this won't happen overnight, but if you give yourself time to grieve and acknowledge your loss, eventually your power will return to you. You will rediscover who you truly are and that is the very essence of spiritual growth.

Reassuring signs

Departed loved ones are capable of sending us messages from the world of spirit. Often these messages take the form of reassuring signs that have unique and personal resonance and it is the deeply personal nature of these communications that gives them such potency and power. There are several reassuring signs in Nicola's story:

Magpie

My dad had cancer of the lungs and brain. He was in a great deal of pain, as you can imagine, and was in and out of hospital for treatment. After a few weeks he was taken into a hospice and then, as his wife wanted him at home, he was provided with a hospital bed in his living room with Marie Curie nurses visiting daily. By now he was virtually blind and unable to care for himself. His recognition of family was almost gone and for him not to really know who I was broke my heart as we had always had a very strong bond between us.

Not too long after he went home he was taken very badly and had to go back to the hospice. We knew that it wouldn't be long for Dad now because prior to these events he had refused any treatment. And then, on 2 May 2010, my brother was at my home assembling some furniture in my son's room when he got a call from the hospice. They asked him to go there and gently asked if I wanted to go with him. You see, I have MS and they/he wanted to protect me, but I decided to go with my brother.

We arrived at the hospice and all of my dad's side of the family were there and, of course, his wife too. Dad was in a coma, and we were told it could be any time. My brother and I looked at Dad just lying there, when all of a sudden he sat up and reached towards the ceiling with a gasp of air. Shocked, I asked my brother, 'What's happening?' He put his arm around me and led me out. They then told us Dad was gone. You can imagine how we all were – floods of tears from everyone.

When I arrived home that day my boyfriend, my mum and my eleven-year-old son were there. I went into the kitchen and after a hug from my boyfriend I stood by the kettle, about to lift it, when I smelled a very delicate fragrance. I didn't recognise it and then it disappeared almost as soon as I smelled it. Then, a day after the funeral, I had another sign. My boyfriend and I were sitting in my living room when a magpie sat on the window ledge and stared through the window at us. Birds don't usually sit there, and I had a strong sense that Dad was behind it.

Just one more thing I want to tell you about. After Dad died I went to stay with my brother, his wife and their little girl. It was the right decision because my brother and I seemed to build an even stronger loving bond. When I came back my boyfriend and I decided to split up. When Dad was very ill my boyfriend had been a huge comfort to me and I do wonder if he was an angel in disguise, to coin a phrase, just to be with me for the time he was sent to be. We were together only four months.

For Nicola, it was a combination of signs – in her case, a delicate fragrance, the timely appearance of a magpie and the ending of a relationship – that gave her a sense of peace, healing and comfort following the death of her father. And I've collected thousands of stories from ordinary people who believe they have experienced unique signs from departed loved ones. Sometimes it is a build-up of meaningful signs, as it was for Nicola, but for other people it may just be one sign. Remember Kerryanne, the musician's story on p. 75? She has another experience to share. For her, that meaningful sign was a single petal. Here's her story:

The petal

I've never been a spiritual person although I've always believed there's some kind of force at work. A few years ago now my grandmother on my mother's side had cancer. I used to go to her house and just chat to her to try and lift her mood. Due to her medication she didn't really eat so I used to try and make her eat something light, normally orange-flavoured jelly. It had to be orange as she was allergic to blackcurrant.

Anyway, she soon afterwards was admitted to hospital and drastically deteriorated within days. She couldn't speak, but surprised us all one day when my brother said to her that he loved her and she replied, 'Love you too, son!' My brother and Gran were really close – he used to live with her and look after her. The whole family used to go up to the hospital every day just to sit with her.

There came a point on 28 April that my mum and uncle said they felt as if the children should leave and go home as it was getting late. So my two cousins, my brother and I went home to stay at my cousins'. We sat and watched DVDs for a while and then early in the morning of 29 April, a petal fell on the floor from a bunch of artificial roses. I didn't know how that could happen and asked my cousins and brother what they thought, but they said it was nothing. I just couldn't let it go though. I said I thought Gran had passed and the petal falling down was her way of saying her goodbyes to us all – they just ignored me.

About an hour later my uncle came in and told us Gran had passed away. I knew then without a doubt that the petal falling was her saying goodbye to us in her own gentle way and even though my cousins and brother still didn't see it, or believe me, I know it was her ... I just know.

Again we return to those three powerful words I hear over and over and over again when reading stories and emails – 'I just know' – and that 'knowing' brings a comfort nothing else can.

In many cases, the timely appearance of a single white feather is enough to convince those who are grieving that a loved one is watching over them. This was certainly the case for Beverley and her sisters:

Tracey

I would like to share my story with you. My dad died two years ago on 15 July from lung cancer. When I got a phone call from my mum at 3.15 that morning to say he had gone, my brother came round to collect me and take me to her house. I gave Mum a big cuddle and said I hoped Tracey, our sister who had died when she was only two and a half years old, would be waiting for him.

Anyway, when the undertakers were removing Dad's body from the house, my sister Carol, my mum and I went out into the back garden. We couldn't bear the thought of him leaving in this way. I again asked if Tracey would be waiting for him and at that exact moment the three of us witnessed a single white feather floating from side to side before it gently settled onto the decking. We all looked at each other and just knew then that Tracey had come to collect her father. Carol said, 'Well, we had him for thirty years. Now it's her turn to have him.'

Another commonly reported phenomenon is clocks or watches stopping at exactly the same time that a loved one passes over. This happened to Tim's father and it gave him, and Tim who tells his story below, quite a shock.

A bit of a shock

My grandpa passed away. It was a sad blessing really as he was ninety-six years old and starting to suffer with dementia. My grandpa believed very much in the afterlife and I believe he sent us a message. Not long after the funeral my dad came round to see me. He told me that the previous day the watch his dad – my grandfather – had given him had suddenly and inexplicably stopped at 7.10 pm, then jumped forward to 7.20 pm. My grandpa had passed away a week previously at 7.20 pm. It gave him a bit of a shock.

Other well-reported signs range from the timely appearance of birds, butterflies, rainbows and clouds, to withered plants flowering, kettles or TVs switching on spontaneously, lights flickering and doorbells ringing, but whatever form the signs take, they all have one thing in common: they provide comfort and reassurance to those who are grieving.

You'll probably have noticed that many of the signs mentioned above are also associated with signs sent by our angels, showing once again, as this chapter draws to an end, how closely related reassuring messages from angels and comforting signs from loved ones in spirit can be. Just as there are countless ways for angels to speak to us, there are also countless ways for loved ones to come back to us from the other side to prove that they have not abandoned us. In the next chapter we'll linger for a while longer with this and explore yet more of these wonderful and reassuring signs from above.

A brilliant new beginning

If you've ever lost a loved one you'll know that it is one of the hardest things anyone will ever have to face emotionally. You'll know that mixed with a sense of loss, grief, loneliness, confusion and emptiness there can also be a hint of anger or resentment at the unfairness of it all. Why did this horrible thing happen? Why me? Why now? There may also be a feeling of anger towards the lost loved one. How could they leave you now? When my mother died, a part of me was furious. I felt she had abandoned me. How could she leave me when I still needed her so very much? But time and time again I've seen how this challenging, complex and emotional journey becomes so much easier to bear when the person who is grieving receives a comforting message or a sign that helps them understand that death is not the end but a brilliant new beginning.

For me, and the ever-growing numbers of people who believe in angels, these reassuring messages from the afterlife offer conclusive proof that there is no such thing as death, only a transition to a new life in spirit.

CHAPTER 6

Angel Calling Cards

God does not die on the day when we cease to believe in a personal deity, but we die on the day when our lives cease to be illuminated by the steady radiance, renewed daily, of a wonder, the source of which is beyond all reason.

Dag Hammarskjold

So far we've seen how angels and the spirits of departed loved ones are always reaching out to us. In rare instances you may see or hear celestial messages, but you are more likely to experience them in the form of intuitive feelings and thoughts or through reassuring signs from the other side or, as I often like to call them, 'angel calling cards'. We've touched on some of these already in the previous chapters, but the collection of stories in this chapter will give you an even deeper understanding of angelic calling cards and, hopefully, encourage you to ask for and notice them yourself.

Life can be stressful and challenging for everyone. Even the most spiritually advanced people feel alone at times and receiving a sign from above can be incredibly reassuring and comforting. Suddenly, we don't feel so alone any more.

Generally, angel calling cards or signs tend to be personally meaningful. They also tend to appear in answer to your heartfelt prayers. You may wonder, as I often used to do, why our heavenly guides approach us in this subtle way and don't just give us more direct assistance when we are in trouble or danger. Occasionally they will intervene in dramatic ways but, as you've seen, more often than not they won't. This is because during our life on earth we must make our own choices so we learn and grow on a spiritual level from the good and the bad. So although they can never intervene without our permission, they can guide us and give us answers, messages or warnings through signs, which if we notice them can point us in the right direction.

Signs are the most common and direct way for angels to speak to us and every day of our lives they are constantly sending them to us. From the moment you woke up this morning to the moment you began reading this book you have already come across a number of signs – all you need to do is believe in them and notice them. Angelic messages are all around you in everyday situations, whether they be big or small, and once you get into the habit of recognising them and listening to them your life can be transformed for ever. Following your signs can help guide you through life, help you make the right decisions and give you a sense that your life has purpose. And the more you ask your angels to send you signs, the more divine calling cards you will receive.

I'm not suggesting here that you search for signs frantically. A lot of people, in the past myself included, may make the mistake of trying to force things. Deliberately seeking out signs can lead to tension and stress, both of which shut down the lines of communication with heaven. You need to be relaxed about it all and notice and listen rather than search or seek out.

The number of possible signs that you could come across is endless but there are some divine calling cards that do tend to appear more than others. In this chapter we'll journey through some of the most frequently reported ways for heaven to send us messages from above. I'm going to begin with a story sent to me by Janice, about one sign no angel book would ever really be complete without: the white feather.

A spiritual woman

I have never been a religious woman. It's just something I have never really thought about, but when it came to losing my mother to leukaemia last year, for the first time in my life I felt the need to believe in something. I loved her more than I loved myself and I just couldn't contemplate life without her. She passed away on 19 March 2009. I was with her at the hospital when she passed. I held her hand and kissed her. She didn't open her eyes but I kept talking to her and one of the things I asked her was to come back and show me a sign.

That same evening I sat alone in my living room with my roommate, Shannon. She had lost her mother when she was fifteen so she knew what I was going through. She told me that I should look out for a single white feather, and the moment – literally the moment – she talked about a feather, one appeared out of nowhere and fluttered down in front of me before settling at my feet. We both could not believe it. We don't have any birds or pets and no feather bedding as my roommate is allergic to that kind of thing.

A few days later I was organising the cremation with my brother and when we were asked if we wanted it to be secular or religious, we both looked at each other and knew that we wanted a priest. When I met the priest at the cremation I got talking to him and told him about the feather. He told me that he had heard many stories about white feathers and other signs and that so many of these things were unexplained and impossible to rationalise. His only explanation was a higher power.

On the morning after the funeral my brother called me to tell me he kept finding white feathers in his house. The following day I was taking an early evening walk when a white feather fell from the sky and followed me along the path a bit. It was fairy windy but when I stopped walking it stopped and let me pick it up. I keep it with me always now, along with that first white feather that appeared the day Mum died.

I haven't found any more white feathers since but I think I've found enough to convince me that my mother is in heaven and that angels are taking care of her.

I still would not describe myself as a religious woman but I would describe myself as a spiritual woman.

Taking into account the number of stories about white feathers that I receive, they are perhaps the ultimate angel calling card and tend to appear when you pray to your angels or ask them for a sign. They can appear on the ground or floating in the air. They usually appear by themselves in unusual locations. You may also notice random feather images on the television or on posters.

Typically the feather is small and stunning white, but heaven will use whatever is available, so the feather can be tiny or large. It will often be thrown or blown onto your path so you can't miss it. However, you do need to believe that angels are communicating with you first, for if you don't, countless angel feathers may cross your path and you will not notice their significance. In the great majority of cases when a person comes across a white feather they know exactly what it means, because it is related to a problem, thought or question they may have been mulling over in their mind. In other words, they immediately understand the connection and their understanding brings reassurance and comfort.

I'm not saying here that white feathers aren't magical – there's a very real possibility they are as they do tend to appear in mysterious places where you least expect them or float down in an unusual, distinctive way – but what I am saying is that it is the impact they can have on a person's life that is the real magic. This is certainly the case for me.

Many people find it hard to believe that a tiny feather can have such a powerful impact or that feathers are divine messages, but for me feathers can be one of the most reassuring signs that angels are all around. Whenever I come across one, for a moment I am mesmerised. However busy I am I will pause to pick it up and caress its softness and feel truly blessed. I always feel a huge inner smile inside me, and there is a knowing, a warm all-embracing knowing that nobody who has ever experienced it can easily deny. If ever I need to be reminded that angels are watching over me I ask for a sign and more often than not that sign is a white feather.

I've lingered here on the subject of feathers because most people these days know that white feathers are common angel calling cards, but they are by no means the only ones. There are a number of other commonly reported angel calling cards. Let's continue here with a story about butterflies sent to me by Shirley.

Butterfly angel

My husband died last year and it's been a rough ride for me. I miss him beyond belief, but something happened last week that gave me hope and made me think that he might not be gone for ever.

It was the first anniversary of my husband's death and I was sitting outside in the garden on the bench where I always used to sit with him and I could feel that lump rising in my throat again. I really didn't want to cry again. Hope this makes sense but I was so exhausted with crying and I begged my husband to send me a sign that he was still close by. A few seconds later this beautiful red and yellow butterfly – I've never seen one so large and so beautiful – settled down on the bench beside me. The two of us sat there for several minutes. I watched the butterfly flap its delicate wings and I could hear my husband laughing gently in the breeze. It was incredible. Eventually, I reached out and touched the tip of one of the butterfly's wings. It just let me stroke it gently, again for a minute or two. Eventually, it rose in the air, hovered a while in front of me and then flew away. I watched it until it vanished in the distance.

I know many people would say that it was just sheer chance a butterfly flew down at that moment. They can't explain so easily why it stayed for so long and even let me stroke it, though. They also can't explain a funny thing that has happened since. Every time I sit on that bench a butterfly comes and sits down with me. It's not the same red and yellow butterfly but a different one. In all the years I sat there with my husband when he was alive, butterflies never flew close to us, but now they sometimes fly in my face to get my attention. I always say hi to them when they do and send my husband my love.

This story really touched me because I can remember on the night of my mother's funeral how a butterfly appeared out of nowhere and remained on my kitchen table. It just didn't move. I put it outside but the next day one that looked exactly the same came back and stayed in exactly the same place. It did make me wonder if this might be Mum's way of saying goodbye.

It can feel very spiritual and mystical when a beautiful butterfly appears and captures our hearts after the recent death of a loved one, or on an anniversary or special day associated with that loved one, or simply when you are thinking about a lost loved one. This Elisabeth Kübler-Ross quote often comes to my mind whenever I think of butterflies and the world of spirit: 'Death is simply a shedding of the physical body like the butterfly shedding its cocoon.'

Another well-reported angel calling card is the timely appearance of a bird. An American Indian lady once told me that in her heritage butterflies and birds were considered to be messengers from the spirit world. Here's Vince's story:

Flutter of wings

After reading your book and what you say about angels on earth I wanted to send in my story. One day last autumn I came home from work but instead of going inside as I normally would I had this strong urge to sit outside, so I went into my back garden.

It was a really beautiful day. I immediately began to unwind as the soft breeze brushed my cheek. I unwound so much that I started to get sleepy, but I was jolted wide awake by what sounded like the flutter of wings, or someone fanning paper near my ears. I looked around but couldn't see any birds. I continued to sit there and started thinking about my sister, Robin. She died when I was ten and she was twelve. She would have been nearly fifty years old now and I wondered – as I have done many times over the years – what she would have done with her life.

Even though she died many years ago the pain of her loss had never really left me. My parents didn't have any more children and a part of me had always longed for a sibling. While I sat there thinking about Robin – that was her name – a little robin redbreast came right up to my feet. I watched it hop around but then it just stopped hopping and stared right up at me with its little brown eyes, brown eyes that reminded me so much of my sister's brown eyes. We looked at each other for some time and then the little bird flew away.

I believe it was all a sign from my sister. There was the obvious link with her name and I had been thinking of her when the bird appeared. Yes, I'm sure there are plenty of other explanations but I'm really not interested in them. All I know is that after my encounter I felt closer to my sister than ever.

As well as the bird in his story, Vince also mentions hearing a 'flutter of wings', but when he opened his eyes there were no birds in sight. I've heard this phenomenon mentioned several other times by people mourning the loss of a loved one. Communications from the other side in the form of butterflies and birds are subtle, but many people tell me that they instinctively recognise them as powerful symbols of love, and they have received great comfort from receiving messages in this form.

For others the sound of birdsong can feel heaven-sent, as was the case for Jemma:

Tuning in

I'm seventeen and there's a lot of pressure in my life right now. I'm close to taking my A levels, but I also have a part-time job, a frail mother to take care of and my younger brothers rely on me for everything. My dad lives close by but never offers to help. There's quite a lot of tension still between him and Mum and I often get caught in the middle. Sometimes I just can't take all that responsibility. I mean, I just want to hang out with my friends sometimes, but I'm never allowed to do that. Everybody relies on me. I'm the capable one.

Two months ago I started to get really worried I would fail my exams and be stuck at home for ever. I got these really bad stomach pains. It became so bad one day that I could barely sit up in class. My tutor was worried and sent me to the school nurse. When I went to the nurse I thought she would give me some pills and send me away, but she sat me down and asked me lots of questions about my home life. After we had chatted for a while she told me to go outside in the school garden and have some 'me' time for an hour. I asked her if I could take my iPod and she said that was fine.

I sat down on the grass in the garden and started to listen to my iPod, but the music wasn't playing loud enough. It was being drowned out by the sound of birdsong. I put the volume up but the birdsong just seemed to get louder. Realising I had lost the battle I pulled out my earphones and decided just to lie down and listen to the birds singing. I'm so glad I did because it was the most peaceful, beautiful and wonderful sound.

An hour later I came back to the nurse and told her I felt so much better, and my stomach pains had completely gone. Just one hour of listening to the birds singing had made me feel like a new person, and since then I have felt much better able to cope with the challenges in my life. I've still got a lot on my plate and my family situation hasn't improved, but I don't let myself get so wound up and exhausted any more. It's like I know how to take care of myself, when to take time out when I need it.

In your book you mention birdsong as a way for angels to speak to us, and I wondered if you thought they spoke to me. I've really been a different, much stronger person ever since.

I wrote back to Jemma and told her that there is a deep and powerful connection between angels and birds and the language of one often reflects the language of the other. Listening with an open heart to birdsong is a truly lovely way to hear angels and invite their comfort and protection into your life. I told her that I truly believed angels spoke to her that day. And, as I was writing this very chapter, I got an email from Jemma telling me that she got the required grades for her first choice of university. Obviously, an hour of listening to birdsong wasn't the key to Jemma's recovery and exam success – that was down to her discipline and hard work – but I do think it acted as a catalyst for positive change.

Clouds are another very well-known angel calling cloud. When you are open and receptive to receiving angel signs you may just notice that the shape of a cloud speaks to you or gives you inspiration and guidance. Joan's story is a lovely read:

A night to remember

I just had to write and tell you about the most beautiful and very special experience I had recently. I was reading one of your books and had just finished the section about angels in the clouds. Even though it was very late, I felt compelled to go to my window, and stayed there with my eyes closed, thinking and praying about what a beautiful sight a cloud in the shape of an angel must be, and hoping it might happen to me.

I don't know how long I stayed there, but when I did open my eyes I just couldn't believe it. There in the sky was a group of angels. They had such beautiful faces and wings and they just shone. They seemed to be floating in and out of the dark, grey clouds. I felt so humble, so happy to be there. A night to remember for the rest of my life, a wonderful night I can't stop thinking about.

I've believed in angels for many years and even more so after I lost my beloved husband in June 2000. He was my soul mate for thirty-three wonderful years. I know he is still around me and that one day we will meet again in a new life.

For some people, like Joan, cloud imagery can be so clear and so dramatic that it can only be interpreted as a sign from above. If you've never spent time cloud-watching, it's something I would certainly encourage you to do. The simple action of raising your head and gazing upwards in awe at the magic, beauty and wonder above you can encourage a much more receptive state. And while we are on the subject of awe, can anything be more magical than the sight of a rainbow? Candice doesn't think so.

End of the beginning

I'm thirty-seven and two years ago I wanted to die. I'm not in that place now but here's something I wrote down at the time for my doctor to read. It will give you an insight into my state of mind.

'I woke up today as I have done every day for the past few months wanting to die. I'm bored with life. My doctor tells me I have clinical depression. I'm taking medication so the pain isn't as deep as it was but I've lost all motivation and sense of purpose. I just don't care about the things I used to – like keeping a tidy house or looking good. I just can't be bothered to make an effort. My two lovely kids are living with my mum now and I can't even summon up the energy to go see them. Some days I don't even want my husband to look at me. I feel so ugly. I do want to laugh again but then I think, Why bother, who cares? Everybody is just so much better off without me.

'It's not even like I have it real bad either. I mean, I don't lack any-thing materially. I live in a good area and all my needs are taken care of by my husband and my parents. I don't have any friends. I don't think people like me. I rarely go out these days. I'm scared of going outside. I just can't see my way outside of this pain and loneliness. I've even stopped going to see my doctor because I am fed up of him thinking I'm crazy. I know that suicide will have a bad effect on my family, especially my kids, but recently I have felt so detached from everyone and everything. I'm getting more and more depressed by the day and everyone's life would be easier if I wasn't here. I used to think, That will never happen to me, but now it is happening to me. If someone tried to kill me, I wouldn't stop them. I do wonder if I am going insane. I just can't be happy. It's not some midlife crisis thing. I genuinely don't think life is worth living.'

It's a depressing read, isn't it, but I think you get the picture. I was at the end of the line and I wanted to end it all. Things came to a crisis point one day when I just couldn't take it any more. I hadn't slept the night before and it was about four o'clock in the morning. I got out of bed, threw some clothes on and headed out of my front door. I didn't know where I was going. I didn't really care. I just walked and walked for hours.

It wasn't until about midday that exhaustion finally got the better of me. I didn't want to stop walking but I couldn't put one foot in front of another. I was miles from home and had no clear idea where I was. There were lots of fields nearby so I just went into one and sat under a tree. At least the exhaustion had shut down the terrible thoughts in my mind. For a while I had peace. I wanted to stay there for ever, but then it started raining and raining hard. The tree gave me hardly any shelter and soon I was soaked.

Eventually the rain stopped and then I started to shiver and my stomach started to howl for food. I curled up into a ball and started to cry and cry. I silently pleaded and cried out for mercy but this time

I didn't find myself longing for the release of death. It's hard to explain really, but the hunger pangs and the cold made me feel intensely alive. I couldn't remember the last time I had felt so hungry. I had to find food. I sat up and as I did so the rain stopped and right in front of me was a beautiful double rainbow. I stopped shivering and my stomach stopped howling. I got up feeling energised and refreshed. I knew then that my guardian angel was with me and always would be and that he, she or it was caring for me.

There was a lot of explaining to do when I eventually got home but that day was the turning point for me. I still get low feelings at times but they are never as desperate and as gut-wrenching as before. Since then I've bought a couple of rainbow paintings and they give me great comfort whenever I look at them. I've stopped wearing black all the time and added a splash of colour to my life. It's symbolic of the way I feel these days. I don't see things in terms of black and white any more. The world I want to live in is full of colour.

I'm in my mid-forties and even now whenever I see a rainbow I stop and stare, just as I did when I was a kid. Rainbows draw me in and I drink them up with all my senses. Such feelings of awe help to connect me with my angels.

Few would deny that rainbows are awe-inspiring, but if you take the time to pause and look, there is so much beauty and wonder in the natural world. From waterfalls to sunsets, from spider webs to dewdrops, there are limitless ways for angels to reveal themselves to us. Indeed, anything that inspires feelings of awe and wonder in you can be a vehicle for celestial beings to communicate their loving presence. The key word here again is awe.

Just as the food you eat nourishes your body, and some foods are better for you than others, so your feelings are 'food' for your connection with your angels. Respect for life, nature and the amazing world we live in, combined with feelings of awe and wonder, are the richest 'foods' to stimulate your spiritual growth.

So far we have discussed natural signs but remember, as we saw way back in chapter one, angels don't limit themselves to the natural world, they can also speak to us through material things. Another well-documented sign that angels can use is coins, typically ones of small value, in usual places. Michele told me about her experience.

Penny from heaven

My daughter died in 1996 from a rare form of meningitis. She was just two years old. I miss her every moment of every day and night. My marriage broke up soon after because we just couldn't cope with the loss. For eight years I stayed single. I had one or two relationships but nothing serious. Then in 2004 I met Jay. We fell in love and got married and in 2005 I fell pregnant. Eight months later I had a beautiful baby girl. Trouble was, I was terrified she would die too. I didn't trust myself to look after her so I put her in day nursery as soon as I could. Two years later I pulled her out and I'll explain why.

It was the anniversary of my first daughter's death and I was feeling very emotional because I couldn't reconcile my feelings for my living daughter with my feelings for my dead daughter. It was impacting my marriage as well and history looked like repeating itself for me when my husband told me he had had enough and was going to file for custody of Clara – that's my daughter's name – because I went to pieces around her. I didn't know what to do. I knew I wasn't being a loving mother but my heart still belonged to Sophie – my first daughter. Letting myself fall in love with Clara felt like a betrayal to Sophie. I couldn't think of a way out.

Anyway, I was coming home from work on the anniversary of Sophie's death, feeling very conflicted, when I decided to take some time out and have a cup of coffee. I went to a coffee bar and ordered my usual latte before finding a seat. Just before I sat down I noticed a sparklingly clean bright penny on the chair. Normally I would have ignored it but it was so bright and clean and shiny I was enchanted by it. I picked it up and had a good look at it. I guessed it had to be brand new as a penny older than a year would never have looked that perfect, but when I checked the date it was 1996.

In an instant the significance of the date hit me. Sophie had died in 1996. Was this some kind of message or sign from her? I put the penny in my pocket and felt my hands trembling as I drank my coffee and in my heart I asked Sophie to help me and show me one more sign. On the way home I kept my eyes peeled for other coins but didn't find any.

I felt a bit foolish when I got home but later that evening Clara came up to me and shoved a penny in my face. I could not believe it. It was a shiny penny dated 1996. I checked my pocket and sure enough the penny wasn't there. It must have fallen out when I got home from the coffee bar. I don't know how, though, as I was wearing fairly tight trousers and it would have been hard for the penny to fall out.

This was the sign I had been looking for all these years, a sign from Sophie that it was OK for me to move on. I wasn't betraying her by bonding with Clara. Quite the opposite, I was honouring her wonderful memory. It didn't take long to get to know my beautiful Clara and show her how much I loved her. I talked to my husband and we agreed that I should work part-time for a few years so I could spend more time with Clara. Today, we are as close as mother and daughter can be, and I have my Sophie to thank for that. She knew I was struggling and she sent me a sign. She lives on in the loving bond between me and Clara. She hasn't died. I can still feel her all around me.

Angels will sometimes use unexpected and highly creative ways to make us pay attention. For example, my angels will often speak to me through the media. If I'm pondering a question or grappling with a problem in my mind I often find that I turn on the TV or radio or go online and without even looking I get answers or a fresh perspective that helps me move forward. It happens most often with songs. I'll go into a shop or turn on the radio in my car and I'll hear a song with the most relevant and helpful lyrics. Bumper stickers on cars, overheard conversations, or even people's T-shirts can also sometimes give me great advice. I'll be thinking about some challenge or question and then I'll glance up and read words that give me the answers I need at the time. If you're thinking this all sounds rather far-fetched, just give it a try the next time you want an answer to some question. You'll be as surprised as Alex was in her story below at what great insight you may come across if you keep your ears, your eyes, your mind and your heart open.

My sign

Two years ago I was in a very negative and abusive relationship. My boyfriend didn't hit me physically but he was extremely critical and always pulled me down. He was draining my energy. I knew it wasn't working but I thought I could change him, make him see how much I loved him and how much I was doing for him. I wanted him to treasure me. All my friends told me to leave him, but I didn't get it. In my mind relationships were for better or for worse. It didn't occur to me that apart from the first few heady weeks, it was all 'worse'.

One night I came home from work and found my boyfriend still in bed. He hadn't worked for the past year and was increasingly turning into a nocturnal creature, getting up at about six pm and staying awake until the following morning. I'd had a really tough day at work and his lifestyle was sucking the life out of me because he expected me to stay up with him. By ten pm I was so tired, all I wanted to do was go to bed and sleep, but he wanted to go out for a drink. As usual I went along with it, but then as we were walking into the bar I got the sign I had been waiting for all my life. Just over the bar was a sign that read, 'Life is a cup to be filled, not drained.'

I just stood there looking at the sign. My boyfriend tried to get me to sit down but I couldn't budge. My guardian angels had set it out for me clearly in bold red writing. I needed to seek out relationships and situations that inspired and uplifted me, not ones that drained the life out of me. I told my boyfriend I needed to pop home to get my purse, but when I got there I packed up all my things and walked out of his flat and his life for ever. It was the best decision I ever made. It felt like a weight had fallen off my shoulders.

Our angels want us to hear them so they create many different ways to give us signs. Lost objects that are miraculously found at crucial moments are another common angel calling card. This is the right place to share Sasha's story with you:

Lost and found

Thirty years ago the most wonderful young man asked me to marry him. He was called William and we hit it off right away. He bought me a stunning engagement ring – close to half a year's wages spent on it, I would guess. I remember the day he gave it to me. It was so romantic. It was snowing and he went down on bended knee in the snow and slipped it onto my finger. It was the most beautiful thing I had ever seen. Of course, I would have loved William even if he had given me a ring out of a Christmas cracker, but on that day with that ring on my finger I felt like a princess.

Every night after I got my ring I would stare at it for several moments before I took it off. It had a stunningly beautiful emerald in the centre and two tiny diamonds either side of it. Green was always my favourite colour. William was thoughtful like that. You'll notice that I speak of William in the past tense, because after nineteen beautiful years together as a married couple he died. It was very sudden and unexpected. He came home from work one day with chest pains and a week later he was gone.

I was lost without him. We weren't blessed with children and I got terribly depressed. I stopped eating and sleeping. I lost a lot of weight and this could well be the reason why I lost my engagement ring. My fingers had got so thin and bony that it must have fallen right off. I used to always wear my engagement ring on top of my wedding ring. William used to tell me to wear them the other way round because there was a danger that it might fall off, but I was convinced that wouldn't happen or I would notice it falling off. It just looked better with the engagement ring sitting on top of the wedding ring.

On the day I lost my ring I had gone to the place where William first proposed. It was snowing as I walked and I relived that intensely happy moment. It was only when I got home that I noticed the ring had disappeared. I retraced my steps and dug around in the snow but it was like looking for a needle in a haystack. I had lost William and now I had lost my engagement ring.

In the days, weeks and months that followed I also lost my love of life. William and I had always been volunteer workers for our local community but I didn't have the will any more. I stopped walking and taking exercise and I stopped keeping up with my friends. I went through the motions at work. I wasn't living at all. I knew I was turning into a bitter old lady but felt powerless to stop it. Then on the day that should have been our twentieth wedding anniversary my house was burgled. Beloved possessions I had shared with William were trashed. Not content with taking my things, the thieves even left a reminder of their visit to me in the toilet. The police couldn't really do anything, except advise me to get stronger locks.

So there I was sitting in a police station waiting for a car to take me to a local hotel for the night, but not really caring what happened to me next, when the most awesome thing happened. A young guy, about the same age as William had been when he proposed to me, came into the station. I was sitting so close to the desk that I couldn't help but overhear the conversation. He said he had been walking his dog on the village green and his dog had started digging and almost swallowed this ring. It was such a beautiful ring that he knew someone must be missing it terribly so he hoped the police could find the owner.

Instantly I got up and it didn't take long to recognise my ring. I had to provide documents of ownership to prove that it belonged to me, but a few days later it was back on my finger where it belonged, only this time sitting underneath my wedding ring for safety. Theresa, you have no idea how it helped me, getting my engagement ring back, on our twentieth wedding anniversary of all days. I really believe my guardian angel wanted me to be reunited with my engagement ring and I really believe William wanted me to be wearing it on our twentieth anniversary. You see, emerald is also the gemstone for twenty years of marriage.

As well as making me feel that William hadn't left me, the incident also helped me re-engage with life and other people. I had been on a very dark path, but that young man's honesty reminded me that there is goodness in human nature. He could easily have tried to sell the ring but he chose to do the right thing. You hear so much on the TV these days but there are still caring, honest and thoughtful people in the world. So you see, it wasn't just my ring that was lost and found, it was my faith in human nature.

I still miss William beyond belief but even though he isn't with me in a physical way, I sense him around me all the time.

Moving on now from objects lost and found to what could very well be the simplest and easiest way, but also the most often ignored or neglected way, to connect with your angels – the world of your dreams. In chapter five we saw how angels can choose to manifest themselves through visions of departed loved ones, but it is important to point out that they can appear in any form imaginable in your dreams. It is not what you see in your dream that is important, but what feelings the dream inspires in you. If a dream leaves you with feelings of awe, love and wonder, and when you wake up you feel more renewed and resolved than when you went to sleep the night before, the source is angelic. If you wake up feeling scared and confused, the message isn't from your angels.

You may wonder how angels can enter our dreams. It's certainly possible that during the dream state, when our analytical left brain is more relaxed and the intuitive, creative right brain more vibrant, we are more open to communication with our angels. It's also possible that heaven-inspired dreams are produced by the aspiring angel inside us all. At the end of the day, I don't think it really matters whether the angels in our dreams originate from within us or from the spirit world around us, because we are all connected and one spirit. What matters most about manifestations of the divine in our dreams is the message of love, comfort and hope they bring.

Adele's short story, below, illustrates this point well, I think.

Shining a light

Last night I was upset before going to bed as I believed there was some information that I had not put on my computer at work. I'm a nurse, and I would have been in trouble, but I dreamt the angels were shining a light onto my computer and telling me I had put the information there. I woke up thinking, If that's true then I'll certainly believe in the angels, and of course it was true, I had put the information on the computer.

As does this one sent to me by Bill.

Drink lots

Keeping fit has always been my number-one priority. I run several times a week, walk lots and weight-train. I hate doctors and usually avoid them at all costs. When I moved I didn't even register with my doctor. I didn't see the need. Then I had this dream about my uncle telling me to drink lots and see my doctor. The dream was so vivid and so clear I just couldn't stop thinking about it. This was a clear message to register with my doctor and have a medical. A month later I was diagnosed with a serious urinary tract infection and put on antibiotics. I was also told to drink lots and lots of water!

Meryl's story below is all about following your dreams.

A dream I once had...

In the late autumn of 1999, I was singing and performing at my local theatre. I had just started writing songs and was thinking of taking it all to a more professional level. One night I had the most spectacular dream ever.

In my dream I woke to find myself in a strange bedroom (which I supposed was a loft conversion) and glanced to my right. There in the most beautiful stained-glass window was a gleaming angel with out-stretched wings shining and glistening with all the colours of the rainbow. A feeling of great peace and overwhelming love soared through me and lingered long after the dream had gone. I was worried that one day I would forget this experience so I rang an artist friend of mine, thinking that if my dream could be interpreted into a painting I would remember it always. He was very moved by my experience. 'Just a moment,' he said and I heard him go and get some paper from his drawer ... he's drawing it already, I thought. 'What did you say when you first rang me?' he asked. 'Imagine all the colours on an angel's wings,' I answered. 'This isn't a painting, it's the first line of your song,' he declared. 'Go and write it.' I did just that, and we performed it for Christmas at our local theatre. It was a huge success.

This song was the start of many for me. My father, whom I have always tried hard to please, suddenly showed an interest in my songs and gave me a cheque for Christmas, and with it I was able to have a music room with equipment and I converted the loft into a bedroom! Music is my life and I think this dream was a sign for me to carry on writing. One of my songs, 'The Journey', has been recorded by John Payonk and you can find it online on YouTube.

I'm going to round off this chapter by talking about one of my favourite divine calling cards – coincidences. The definition of a coincidence is a chance or random event, but to those who experience coincidences they can feel like something much bigger than that. They can feel like the hand of destiny. Angels guiding our life choices through coincidences isn't the same as them running our lives. Remember, angels will never interfere with our free will, but they can use coincidences to help guide us onto a path that can lead us to happiness and fulfilment.

I guess you could say that a great majority of the stories in this book are about the magic of coincidences, and that is because coincidences are perhaps one of the favourite ways for angels to speak to us. Paying attention to coincidences, even if they are subtle or appear trivial at the time, can have a life-transforming effect because they do seem to suggest there is a higher power at work in our lives.

If you still aren't convinced, may I remind you of the famous story of seventeenth-century scientist Isaac Newton. It was the apparently trivial coincidence of an ordinary, everyday apple falling from a tree in his mother's garden at the exact same moment he was pondering the huge 'why' questions of nature that instantly helped him formulate the law of gravity. I believe a higher force was involved. Angels wanted to open Newton's brilliant mind to how beautiful and orderly the world is – and to do this an apple was chosen, perhaps to contradict the disorder and sin that had marked the world when an earlier apple was plucked in the Garden of Eden.

In the years I have been collecting angel stories I never cease to marvel at how apparently trivial events, like an apple falling from a tree or a missed train or a lost object found at the perfect moment, can have a powerful effect on people's lives. The coincidences that touched the lives of the people in the next few stories may not have had the universal effect of Newton's falling apple but, as they all explain below, from a personal point of view the impact was profound.

I'll jump right in here with this story from Helen.

Walk in the park

My youngest son Steve was four and a half years old. He had just started infant school and because he was one of the youngest in his group he was only allowed to attend part-time for the first term. So I would collect my son at lunchtime.

We had a huge and beautiful park nearby, which was surrounded by a cycle path. On this particular day I decided to walk through the park because it was a short cut to the school. As I entered the park a horrible feeling just washed over me. I noticed that there was no one else there – I really felt alone. Then I heard someone walking behind me, so I picked up my pace, but I felt like I was on a treadmill. I knew I had at least ten minutes to get to the other side of the park. I started to battle with thoughts of what could happen. I wanted to get to my son. I knew that Steve would be waiting for me. I was so scared.

I remember the feelings I had were so strong that I prayed to God. If this person walking behind me was going to hurt me, I didn't care what he did to me, as long as I could walk away and collect my son.

Suddenly, three ladies came into view and crossed my pathway. I never felt so relieved and happy to someone. The footsteps disappeared very quickly and no one walked past me. I felt a calm and relaxed feeling enter my body, and I knew I was safe. I collected Steve from school, and from then on have always taken the longer and safer route to collect him.

Sure, you could say it was pure coincidence that three ladies appeared at exactly the right time for Helen, but whenever I read stories like this I find it hard not to think that coincidences are the work of angels done by people – more about that in the next chapter.

Kylie sent me this next account. I'm slotting it in here because again it illustrates that what many might dismiss as pure coincidence could very well be the work of a guardian angel.

All for a reason

I am a childcare worker. One day I had just put a baby down for a nap – she was about seven months old. I tucked her in and left the room. Then I sat in the main room with the other children and began to do some tasks. I heard the baby I had put in her cot crying for a few seconds but then the crying stopped. I don't know why, but I had a strong urge come over me to go and check on this child. I put down what I was doing and went in and checked on the baby.

When I got in the cot room, the baby had somehow pulled out her sheet and must have rolled around in her cot for a bit as the sheet was wrapped around her face and neck. I took the sheet off and the baby looked at me. Thankfully, she was just fine.

I really believe someone was sending me a message to let me know something was wrong. It was just too much of a coincidence that I got this urge to check on her. Even another carer said, 'I think someone was watching out for her.'

I am also a true believer that things happen for a reason, for example we get delayed and avoid something happening to us. Two examples for me are:

My partner and I were going to a party and on the way there, there had been a car crash. I believe that maybe we did something that took extra time when we were getting ready, otherwise it could have been us in the crash. Another incident was when we were getting ready for a motorbike ride, but my partner realised he had forgotten to put chain lube on the chain, so he stopped to put some on. On the way to our destination there was another crash and the road was blocked off. We had to do a huge detour. I believe that if we hadn't delayed our start to put on the chain lube we may have been in the crash also.

Helen, whose story is below, also believes things happen for a reason – even unpleasant and inconvenient things like delays or bouts of illness.

The miracle of life

I was married and we had a son who was eighteen months old, and my husband and I were trying for our second child. Each month would go by and I would receive disappointment and heartache, and this had been going on for at least a year. We didn't seek medical help as we already had a child, so I began to accept we couldn't have another child and to be grateful we had a beautiful and precious son.

My husband had a friend who started his own gym business, so my husband thought it would be a good idea for us to join and do something together to take our mind off things. We would have a hobby we could enjoy together. Our first session was due to start in a week. We organised for our son to spend the day with my nan while we went to the gym. For the first time in ages I started to enjoy life again and have something to think about apart from getting pregnant.

The trouble was I never really got to the gym. I found that each time

I was due to spend a day at the gym either myself or my husband had a heavy cold or an upset stomach so we had to cancel. The following day the illness would pass. It was crazy. This one-day sickness thing before going to the gym went on for about four weeks. Then I started to feel unwell for longer periods of time. The smell of alcohol turned my stomach. My mother-in-law suggested that I should do a pregnancy test. I did and I couldn't believe the result. I was pregnant, which then got confirmed by my doctor.

I believe that if I had carried on at the gym and trained intensively with weights as planned I would have lost my second son. So I do believe that I had my guardian angel looking after me and protecting my baby.

I agree with Helen. In addition to my own experience of coincidences, over the years I have seen and read enough angel stories to convince me one hundred per cent that things really do happen for a reason. At the time we may not make sense of things, but often when we look back we can see there was a reason and a plan. Perhaps years ago you broke your heart over the ending of a relationship, but now you look back and count your blessings that it ended when it did. Or perhaps you applied for a job and didn't get it but with the hindsight of age and experience you can see that it really wasn't the right job for you.

Think about your life now and the important people in it and how accidental or by chance your first meeting with them might have been. If you had not gone to that party, or applied for that job or taken that train, you might never have met them. There is so much chance involved in relationships starting up that if you look back on your life it can sometimes really feel like a higher force brought you all together.

So the next time you find yourself stunned by a chance meeting or coincidence, don't be too hasty to dismiss it all as mere chance or randomness in a chaotic universe. Even modern science is beginning to come around to the idea that there are subtle but discernible patterns to chaos. Take the miracle of DNA or the human circulatory system or the intricate design of a snowflake: there is nothing random here, just a perfect design and an unexplained intelligence in which everything has its place, function and purpose. And could it not be the same for our lives?

We may not see it or understand it but we can trust that everything happens for a reason and has its place, function and purpose. And what better evidence for this higher power could there be than the magic of coincidences? Also, what better way to live your life than with deep respect and awe for everything that happens in your life? Even something as trivial as forgetting your keys or missing a train or deciding where to do your shopping, because – you never know – that apparently trivial decision, that apparently confusing or frustrating delay or detour, could well transform your life for ever.

Notice what happens next

I hope this chapter has made it clear that there are countless different ways for angels to send us reminders that they are always close by. They don't just appear in life-or-death situations, they can appear at any time in our daily lives and teach us a great deal if we open ourselves up to them. Remember, feathers and clouds aren't the only angel calling cards you need to look out for. They can speak to you in ways that are highly personal and unique to you. Once again, there really is no right or wrong way to experience them and you don't need to be psychic, clairvoyant or a medium either. Like love, angels can be experienced by everyone.

The next time you want to feel comforted or reassured, all you need to do is ask and then notice what happens next. You may see a butterfly or an intriguing shape in the clouds, or you may have a profound dream or flash of intuition that can point you in the right direction. Remember, one of their favourite ways to chat to you is through meaningful coincidences. For example, you may get this urge to turn right instead of going straight ahead and you then bump into an old friend, or you may find that you can't get the lyrics of a song out of your head and these lyrics have a special message for you. They may whisper to you to check your watch and you notice that it is 11.11, the symbol of angelic love and protection. Be open and receptive to the messages that surround you every day and you will soon hear angels in your own unique way.

When you ask your angels for a sign, or divine calling card, you can speak to them out loud or, as many people today prefer to do, you can speak to them in your mind and heart during periods of quiet reflection. Your angels can hear your thoughts as well as your spoken words and you can speak to them any time, anywhere. You can speak to them right now. All they are interested in is the words your heart is saying. Simply believe in them and trust them, ask them to speak to you.

Angels are always with you. No matter how alone or abandoned you feel, you are surrounded by them. Just ask for a sign and when you notice it, trust it with an open heart, because it is through your heart, without the need for any words, that your angels will first speak to you and you will first speak to them.

Just ask them to send you a sign and then listen carefully to find out what happens next.

CHAPTER 7

The Promise

Rather than a soul in a body, become a body in a soul.

Gary Zukav

All you need to do is ask your angels for help.

However, many people find that difficult. I'm not very good at it all, and I suspect that many of you reading this may struggle also. How many times have you told people you were fine when they asked, when they opposite was true? How many times have you silently suffered or said you could cope because you didn't want other people to feel obliged or to go out of their way for you? I used to think that asking for help was a sign of weakness or failure. I felt much more comfortable being the one who offered the help; receiving it was much more complicated.

It is our birthright to ask for what we need and trust that someone in our lives will be there for us, but for all too many people today the simple act of receiving help from others is a problem. We feel guilty for not being able to take responsibility for ourselves and find it virtually impossible to open up and admit we can't cope and need someone there for us.

We just keep soldiering on with a forced smile, but what I hope the stories in this chapter, and indeed this whole book, will show you is that even if you don't want to admit you need help, or think you need assistance, there are times in your life when asking for help is not the weakest but the strongest thing you can do. It takes a very strong person to open themselves up in a vulnerable way and ask. And when you ask, the most incredible thing happens: an angel will come your way, a sign will cross your path and you will be given the help you need. Being there is the promise your angel made to you when you were born. But first you have to open yourself up and ASK.

There will be moments in all our lives when we need to learn the crucial soul lesson of asking for help. Sometimes we need to ask our friends, loved ones or other people for that help, and sometimes we need to ask for divine assistance to help us cope. Whether the help is human or divine, the important thing is that if you need help you ask for it, and know you deserve it by virtue of the fact that you are a human being in need.

So far in this book you've read many stories about people who found themselves in situations where they were truly out of their depth. They realised there was nothing they could do. They were vulnerable, but in their moment of weakness they discovered an open door to heaven in their hearts and this newfound openness and willingness to trust in a higher power gave them the strength they needed to cope or move their lives forward again. In other words, in their moment of need when their hearts were crying out for help they let heaven help them. Divine assistance generally came to them in the form of angel signs, stunning coincidences or visions and whispers from above, but in this chapter you'll see that divine assistance doesn't necessarily have to come in 'unexplained' ways – sometimes it can manifest through the words or actions of other people.

Sometimes when we need help, the simplest way to encounter an angel is to let them talk to us through other people. Wendy's story illustrates this point so well.

All the difference

For two years solid, I suffered major depression. Social anxiety was a lot of that. It wavered between suicidal and just feeling like hell. And still, I felt guilty about asking for help. Part of me felt like I was somehow exaggerating everything to get attention. Part of me felt I should fix it myself. Part of me hoped someone would help me, without my doing anything. Part of me felt that I would hurt those close to me if I told them.

Then one day everything changed. I was walking home with a heavy shopping bag, feeling pretty low. The bag burst and everything fell all over the place. Normally, I would have scrambled around trying to pick everything up but I felt so listless and depressed I couldn't even be bothered to do that. I must have stood there for a good few minutes just staring at the broken bag and the contents scattered all over the ground. Lots of people walked around me nervously, but then this little old lady stopped and asked me if I needed help. I didn't have the energy to say or do anything. I just stared at her and shrugged my shoulders. I thought she would move on like all the others, but instead she slowly and carefully bent down and started picking things up and putting them in a plastic bag she had pulled out of her handbag. Seeing her on her hands and knees like that snapped me out of my paralysis. I told her to stop. She didn't listen. She just continued picking everything up. I told her again to stop but she wouldn't.

I started to get angry. I don't know why. Here was this lady picking everything up for me, helping me, and I was angry with her. It hit me right in the heart and I started to cry. The lady had finished packing by now and got up and she just put her arm around me and told me to 'cry it out'. I think I must have cried for a good five minutes in the street. Eventually, when my tears dried up she gave me a fruit pastel and told me to keep my blood sugar up. I started to apologise over and over again for my behaviour but she told me that everyone feels vulnerable sometimes and asking for help was nothing to be ashamed of.

We said our goodbyes and I had never felt better. I thanked her from the bottom of my heart for her kindness. I don't know who she was or if she was an angel in disguise but she made all the difference. From that moment on it became clear to me that I really did need to ask for help. I went to my doctor and was diagnosed with clinical depression. I'm currently getting a lot of help. I'm not out of the hole, but I do know where the footholds are now.

The reason I'm sending my story is because I really would like you to share it with others to show that if you feel depressed or alone or vulnerable you need to ask for help. You need and deserve it. If it's got to the point where you're thinking you need to tell someone, DO IT! The fact it's that serious proves you're not just creating drama. It is important that you do not keep this to yourself. It took the selfless actions and thoughtful words of a stranger to teach me that important lesson. I truly believe she was guided to me by a higher power.

We constantly tell ourselves that we don't deserve help – but we often forget that there are people who will gladly help when we're in need (or even when we're not). Admitting you can't do something and being willing to accept the help of others is how we learn, it's how we grow – it's the openness of heart that defines life in spirit.

Ignatius also believes that he encountered people who were guided into his life by a higher power.

Ministering angels

My family and I were going to watch a late-night blockbuster at a movie house, and we were getting there from different directions. They were coming directly from home, and I was coming from elsewhere. As I drove into the parking lot, the attendant told me that my left rear car tyre was getting flat. I scrambled out and collected tools from the boot. Just then the entire area suffered a blackout; it was pitch dark.

In moments a car pulled up beside mine. Four young men in their early twenties stepped out. They kept their headlights on and came directly to me, offering to replace the flat tyre with the spare one I had in the car. Very quickly they finished the task. I thanked them profusely, but they shrugged off the good deed as though it were really nothing. Although I move around the city a lot and interact with many young people in different parts of the city, I have not met any of the four Good Samaritans. Who were these ministering angels?

I've been sent quite a few stories like this about mysterious strangers, or as I like to call them 'earth angels', who mysteriously appear in moments of crisis or need and are impossible to trace afterwards. Jane's story falls into this earth angel category.

Just breathe

Fifteen years ago I was driving to a party down a fairly busy main road. One moment I was humming along to songs on my radio and the next a van suddenly reversed into the road and I hit it head on. My car spun out of control and I ploughed into a tree. While my seat secured my body, my airbag didn't inflate and my head continued to travel forwards at fifty or so miles per hour. I heard something crack in my back and went into shock. I just couldn't move a muscle and my hanging head was blocking my windpipe and making it impossible for me to breathe. For what seemed like an eternity I just sat there. I had always wondered as a kid what the final minutes would be like if you knew death was very close.

I watched my hands slowly change colour. I didn't feel any pain, just numbness. I felt sure I was going to die, but then the door opened and a man's face appeared. I can still remember him vividly to this day. His skin was very dark and he had sparkling green eyes. I felt so relieved to see him. Without saying a word he gently lifted my head and told me to 'just breathe'. With my head lifted I was able to breathe again. I felt life returning to my body and could wriggle my fingers and toes. The guy held me in this position for what must have been at least ten or fifteen minutes. He must have been very strong and it was the most reassuring thing to have his arms around me. I tried to speak but he shook his head as if to say, 'Save your energy.' Eventually I heard the welcome sound of an ambulance and he gently, ever so gently rested my head back and left moments before the paramedics arrived.

I was taken into hospital and mercifully made a full recovery – I had a broken arm, several broken ribs and cracked vertebrae and a serious case of whiplash. The van driver didn't fare as well and had to stay in hospital for the best part of a year. As for the amazing man who saved my life by stopping me from suffocating, I've never been able to trace him. The paramedics didn't see him leave, and his presence at the scene of the accident was not written up in my medical report. To all intents and purposes he didn't exist, but I am in no doubt that he was real. I'm in no doubt that he saved my life.

Was the stranger who saved Jane's life a Good Samaritan? If he was, why did he disappear seconds before the paramedics arrived? This poignant story has all the hallmarks of a classic guardian angel story: the helpful, comforting and expertly-trained-for-the-situation stranger who appears and then vanishes inexplicably.

Jane also speaks of her enormous sense of relief when she saw the man's face, even though he was no paramedic and a complete stranger to her.

Something similar may have happened to me several years ago. I was waiting with my two-year-old daughter and four-year-old son at a bus stop when a couple of drunken men started to harass us. I was backed into a corner, and with a double stroller it was hard for me to move away from them quickly. As their body language became more menacing and threatening, I glanced at the cars flashing past in the street and prayed for someone driving past to notice what was going on.

Moments later, a blue limo pulled up on the opposite side of the road. I remember thinking that I hadn't seen a blue limo before. The door of the car opened and a blonde, fair-skinned woman in a dark blue suit leaned out and said quietly, 'Leave her alone.' The drunken men turned away from me and started to walk towards the car, at which point the woman closed her door and drove off. The two drunks kept stumbling along behind her as if they were in a trance. I watched them walk away into the distance. I kept hoping the woman would come back and offer us a lift, because it took another twenty minutes before the bus arrived, but she never did. Whether the woman in the car was an angel or a human guided by an angel I'm not sure, but I have never forgotten her, or her shiny blue limo.

Was the woman in the car an angel, or unconsciously guided by an angel? Her impact on the thugs was certainly out of the ordinary because their behaviour changed dramatically afterwards. Although they were drunk they also suddenly looked scared, which made me wonder what it was that they experienced. Whether she was or not, she will always be a heavenly helper to me because I believe she saved me and my children from a possible assault.

Over the years I've read a lot of wonderful stories that have convinced me that sometimes angels do save lives while in the guise of other people. These people may not be aware that they are being guided by angels, but for the person who experiences their help, compassion and selfless bravery they are truly heaven-sent. Some of these stories feature in the media. There is so much negative news in the press these days, but if you take your time you can find hidden and inspiring gems like these.

August 2009: The parents of a boy who fell beneath a Tube train praised the 'angel' commuter who saved his life. Benjamin Nelson-West, four, slipped into the gap between the train and platform at Acton Town station. A man then threw himself on to the platform and hauled Benjamin out seconds before the train pulled away.

May 2010: Two young men heroically rescued a stranger who had fallen into a frozen lake in Watermead Country Park, Leicestershire, while police were ordered not to go on to the ice.

July 2010: Sharon O'Shea described how a stranger saved her baby, who was trapped in a top-floor flat of a tower block in

Kingston-upon-Thames, south-west London, after a fire broke out.

It's incredibly uplifting to read stories like this because they remind us of the courage and selflessness that resides in our fellow humans. Dramatically saving other people's lives isn't what I'm really highlighting here, though – because sometimes if you aren't trained or able to protect yourself, intervening when another person is in trouble may backfire – what I want to highlight is that we all have the potential within us to be guardian angels to one another. We are all so much more courageous, selfless and strong than we believe ourselves to be.

Wouldn't it be wonderful if we could trust our hearts more and do more good or helpful things for others, not just for the people we know and love but for people we don't know? I remember once how comforted I felt when a complete stranger gave me an umbrella when it was bucketing down with rain and I was standing waiting in a shop door front. She told me not to worry as she had another umbrella in her bag and dozens more at home. And then when my kids were very small there was this wonderful man who packed all my shopping for me when they were playing up at the supermarket checkout. And the time when I was a teenager and trying to buy a ticket with a twenty-pound note but the bus driver refused to give me one because I didn't have any change. I started to panic, but a lovely lady intervened and paid for me. I could cite many examples of random kindness from strangers that made a huge difference to my day, and knowing how reassured and comforted their actions made me feel, I do try my very best to do the same for others. I've found it's a very fulfilling and uplifting way to live.

What is the kindest thing a stranger has done for you or said to you? I really hope you can think of a few examples. If you can't, one of the surest ways to attract the love and kindness of others is to spread some love and kindness yourself. It doesn't have to be anything dramatic, sometimes just holding a door open for the person behind you is enough to lift someone's spirits. What's the nicest thing you have ever done for a stranger?

Sometimes it's not what you do, but what you say that can make all the difference. Why not lend others simple words of encouragement, kindness and hope that can help them feel as if they have been touched by angels? Steve's story below demonstrates the awesome power of a few well-chosen words.

The first time

The best advice I ever got was when I became a father for the first time. My wife had had a prolonged and painful twenty-hour delivery and given birth to a little boy. The relief was incredible, but when the midwife handed my son to me I just felt a rising tide of panic. I was really grown-up now. I was responsible for another human being. I was petrified.

My wife was exhausted, and after a brief cuddle I left her alone with our son. The midwife told me to go get a cup of tea and some rest myself but I was really out of it. I wandered out of the delivery suite and sat in the waiting area, trying to take it all in. I'm not sure if was the dark circles under my eyes, or the look of absolute shock on my face, but this older guy sitting close to me started to chat to me and asked if it was my first child.

I told him that indeed it was my firstborn. He told me that it never got any easier. He had fathered three children himself and his daughter was going to give birth any day now to his grandchild. Realising he was very much a pro when it came to raising kids, I shrugged my shoulders and asked him if he could give me any advice. The guy took a minute to gather his thoughts and then said something I will never forget. He told me to ignore all those people who would tell me it would be better when my baby was on solids, or when my baby slept through the night or when he went to school. He told me to enjoy every moment of it, even the tough times, and never wish it to go faster to get to a better time.

Then he told me the saddest thing. He told me that he had lost one of his children, a little girl aged three, and he would give anything to have her tiptoeing down at night when she should be asleep in bed. He said I should drink in every moment of their precious childhood and enjoy it all, even the tough parts.

My son is twelve now and I also have two little girls, aged seven and three. Now, people who know me will no doubt tell you that I have done my fair share of moaning, and my kids can drive me crazy at times, but I like to think that I have also drunk everything in and, when things aren't going to plan, put it all in perspective.

I never saw that guy again but his words had a positively angelic impact on me as a new father. I got lots of advice from doctors, nurses, family and friends, but his was the advice that made the most sense to me.

Clearly the man in Steve's story chose his words of advice well. He dug deep inside himself and spoke from his heart – the place where angels live. A few simple words also changed Gail's life. Here's her story.

You are loved

My son was in prison for close to two years for assaulting a guy during a fight outside his local pub. He was my only child and seeing him self-destruct like that cut right through me. Being a single parent I blamed myself. I sank deep into depression, split from my partner and couldn't see the point of anything any more. I also felt incredibly alone. All my friends faded away when they heard about what my son had done. I'm sure they blamed me, because I was blaming myself.

The only thing that kept me going was knowing I needed to be there for my son when he came out; I was the only person he had on the outside and he needed me to help him deal with his anger management issues. I got some advice from the prison and probation service, but not nearly enough. On the day before his release I was nervous. I wasn't sure if I could cope. To clear my head I went for a walk in the park and as I was walking, this woman – she looked about my age – came up to me and said, 'You are loved.'

At first, I thought she was a Jehovah's Witness or something, so I told her I wasn't religious. She said she wasn't either, but she had seen me walk many times in the park and I always looked so sad, as if I had the weight of the world on my shoulders. She just wanted to tell me that having faith in the forces of love, goodness and peace could turn my life around. Then she said goodbye and wished me luck.

If only it could be that easy, I thought as I walked home, but just thinking about what that woman had said, especially 'you are loved', really began to make a difference.

I collected my son from prison the following day. It's early days yet but I'm coping much better than I thought I would, and so is he. I'm not completely there yet, and I have my fair share of low days, but what always pulls me out of them is this growing sense that I am somehow loved and protected from above.

Angels will sometimes place people in our lives to give us encouragement, love or hope, or to say the right words at just the time we need them, or when we feel life isn't going to plan. Did a simple heartfelt word, piece of advice or helpful conversation ever set you on a different path or help you get back on track?

Again this was once the case for me. About seven or eight years ago I was going through a phase when I really wanted to just concentrate on my family and my angel writing, but I couldn't because I needed to take a lot of research jobs to help pay the bills. My salvation came from the most unlikely source, through a few simple words spoken by my brother. I met up with him for a coffee and started complaining about my long to-do list and all the things I should be doing instead of drinking coffee with him.

He looked at me and said, 'You don't have to do anything, you are choosing to do all these things.' I disagreed with him instantly, but then he reminded me that I chose to go to work because I loved my family and wanted to provide for them. I chose to clean the house because I liked to have a clean home. I needed to replace the word 'should' with the word 'choose', as strictly speaking I did have a choice. I could quit working and let my children suffer. I could leave my house dirty; nobody was forcing me to clean.

My brother was right, of course. 'Should' is an incredibly disempowering word and substituting it with 'choose' or 'could' can make a huge difference. Switching the word 'fear' with the word 'excitement', the word 'problem' with the word 'opportunity' can give you a similar rush of adrenaline. It really isn't enough to think positively and hope for the best. To see positive changes in your life you need to change your words – so that your words can change your mind, your actions and your life for the better. Words are like the rudder on a moving boat. They can change the direction of your life.

What have you been saying about yourself and others lately? Make a promise to yourself to try to use words that energise, motivate and attract angels to heal, guide and inspire you.

Think about it: hundreds of words pour out of our mouths each day as our thoughts, opinions, judgements and beliefs are freely expressed. Often, however, we are oblivious to the positive or negative influence these words have on us and the people around us. Thoughts make an impression on your mind but words leave a lasting imprint. So, instead of moaning, self-pitying, swearing or spiteful words, make a promise to yourself today to use only empowering words: words that build you up instead of pull you down. If you don't believe me, try saying the word 'angel' or the words 'love', 'faith' and 'hope' several times. You will soon understand what I mean.

I've digressed a little here from this chapter's theme of angels speaking to you through the words and actions of others, but I just wanted to remind you that you also have the power to be an angel to yourself and to others, not just through the things you do, but also through the things you say. To return now to stories about the power of some simple, well-chosen words, don't think that these words always have to be intensely profound and serious. Sometimes your angels will reach out to you through humour, as they did in this charming story sent to me by Rob below.

Look on the bright side

I started to lose my hair in my late teens. I could hide it then but in my twenties and then my thirties it got worse and worse. For a good ten years I tried to disguise my hair loss as best I could by combing my thinning hair a certain way. Then I started to invest big-time in a toupee. My sister used to hate me wearing it and told me time and time again just to accept I was losing my hair. That was something I simply wasn't ready to do.

The day my attitude to going bald changed started like any other day. I went to work as usual and had to interview a number of candidates for a position within my company. The first guy I interviewed was also losing his hair, but unlike me he didn't attempt to disguise it with a toupee. It was raining that day and my toupee had got very soggy. During the interview I could feel drips of water from it running down my face and my head was getting very itchy. I was angry with myself for not having put my umbrella up to protect my toupee. On the way to work I hadn't thought it was raining very hard, but when I got to work I soon realised I was drenched.

The guy must have noticed my discomfort, because he smiled broadly and in a very deadpan, self-deprecating way said, 'That's one of the many benefits of me being bald, you know – I can always tell first when it's raining.'

I don't know whether it was the way he said it, or just that I was in a good mood, but I couldn't stop laughing. I peeled off my soggy toupee to the great delight of the guy I was interviewing. When we had stopped laughing he told me that he used to wear toupees, but his wife hated them so he stopped.

And three years on from that memorable interview I have to agree that going bald really comes down to how you feel about it. My life became much more enjoyable after I stopped caring about losing my hair. I needed a good dose of laughter to help me see that.

I don't think this is an angel story but I wanted to send it to you because you often talk about how angels can manifest in the most unusual ways, and if I look back I can see that this guy helped liberate me from my anxieties about going bald. He was offered the job but declined it for an offer elsewhere, which again makes me think that I was meant to meet him on that rainy day. He came at just the right time in my life and whenever someone like that comes along it can feel like a gift from heaven.

People often think that laughter and spirituality don't mix, but quite the opposite is true, as long as the laugher doesn't cause anyone to suffer or feel humiliated. Remember that famous Chesterton quote, 'Angels can fly because they take themselves lightly'? Seriousness of purpose and a sense of humour can go together. The angels love to laugh and they love to hear you laugh, so don't take yourself too seriously. I've been sent many stories that prove to me beyond doubt that heaven has a sense of humour. Andrea's story is a fine example, showing that whenever there is innocent laughter and fun, angels are always close by.

Oh my God!

When Dad died last year I missed him deeply. I'm a real Daddy's girl and we shared so much laughter together. About a month before he died, when he got very ill and weak, he told me not to be sad and to remember the good times. If I was too sad he would find some way of coming back and reminding me to smile again. I tried to be brave, but the thought of moving forward with my life without him was unbearable. To make matters worse, he died the evening before my twenty-first birthday. I should have been celebrating and having fun but instead I was crying and mourning.

For three days I wore myself out. Just when I thought I was out of tears they came back again. It was even worse on the day of the funeral. Mum and I were in the car directly behind the hearse. Just knowing his body was so close and I couldn't hug him hurt so much. When we got to the church I walked beside his coffin as it was carried in. I needed to feel close to him. Eventually Mum coaxed me away and I sat down hugging her and sobbing. Mum tried to calm me down but I could feel myself getting hysterical. I wasn't ready to say goodbye to Dad. I needed to know that he was still there for me.

The organ started playing and I looked around and saw the vicar walk solemnly towards the altar. I noticed that he had a really odd haircut, the closest to a mullet I have seen this century and I kind of got oddly transfixed by it. He walked past me and then he must have tripped on his robe or something because he fell flat on his face, and everyone heard him shout, 'Oh God!' It shouldn't have been a funny moment but it so was.

The deeply embarrassed vicar hastily got up and tried to carry on. I tried to stop giggling but when I looked at Mum she was cracking up too, as were most of the people around me. In that moment I knew that Dad hadn't forgotten about me, hadn't left me. Here was the sign that he had promised. He was telling me in his own way to remember the laughter and to keep on laughing. And I can still feel him around me, you know, whenever I have a good laugh. I still miss him but he's with me whenever I smile.

Andrea's story shows that anything or anyone that helps to raise your spirits is an angel in disguise, but of course it is not just the words or actions of other people that can help raise our spirits, sometimes angels will take the form of our beloved pets.

You're probably quite familiar with stories about dogs and cats, the most popular household pets, saving, healing or changing lives for the better, but animals of all kinds can have a remarkable healing effect. That's why I chose to include this story reported in the media in December 2009:

The life-saving elephant

Five years later, there are many tales from the tsunami of extraordinary survival and heroism. But perhaps the most amazing is that of a baby elephant saving a child. Elephants, or chang as they are known in Thailand, are greatly admired there for their intelligence and strength. And that was certainly needed on the day the tsunami struck. Virtually every day, baby elephants from the Sheraton Grande Laguna in Phuket entertain tourists on the beach. And they happened to be there when the tsunami struck.

During the Christmas holidays in 2004, Amber was enjoying the trip of a lifetime in Phuket, Thailand, with her mother and stepfather. Along with the dream hotel and stunning beaches, there was an added attraction for Amber – a four-year-old elephant called Ning Nong and his handler, Yong, who were regular visitors to the hotel. Amber bonded with the young elephant and spent most of her time playing with him on the beach.

As Amber and her parents enjoyed a Christmas Day barbecue on the beach, there was little sign that anything out of the ordinary was about to happen. But in the early hours of Boxing Day, the continental plates collided. As the killer wave rushed towards the beach, Ning Nong raced away just in time, carrying Amber safely on his back. Others were not so fortunate, and Ning Nong's quick reaction made the difference between life and death. Wildlife vet Roman Pizzi believes that the girl and the animal had formed a deep connection thanks to the hours they had spent playing together and it is this deep bond that could well have saved her life.

The elephants have since become symbols of Phuket's recovery and continue to return to the beach and the sea every day.

This next story wasn't reported in the media, but this does not make it any the less miraculous. It was sent to me by Donna.

Equestrian miracle

I grew up on the family farm so I was used to being around animals and I had a real bond with my horse, Princess. When I was about ten years old my uncle came to visit and he had this really huge scary dog – I think it was a pitbull. He always kept the dog on a lead and I was told not to approach it, but on that day when I was mucking out Princess in her stables the dog somehow got loose. I heard barking and a commotion and saw the dog rushing towards me. There was nowhere for me to run. I was so scared. I was small for my age and just curled into a terrified ball to protect my face.

The dog leapt on me but then I heard a thud and an almighty yelp, and the dog fell off me. Princess had moved forward and kicked the dog with her hoof. I really believe that without Princess kicking like that I would have been killed. She saved my life. I had only a few minor scratches, but the pitbull had a serious stomach wound. He recovered but was permanently muzzled after that.

The vet told me that he had heard of dogs coming to the rescue like that but not horses. This was something new. I don't know if other people have had similar experiences, but whether it was something new or not, it was a miracle for me. I've never forgotten it and twenty-five years later my love affair with horses continues. I own my own stables and am a registered riding instructor.

I've got files of heart-warming stories about animals bringing a glimpse of heaven into the lives of their owners. I've also got just as many stories about pets who have come back to reassure or visit their owners from the other side, proving that love in whatever shape or form it takes transcends death. Sadly, I'm running out of word count here so I can't share any more animal angel stories – that will have to wait until next time – but I just couldn't finish this book without mentioning animals. Like angels, animals simply love us and watch over us in this life and the next, and their unconditional devotion really can heal and transform lives in wonderful ways.

I also couldn't close this chapter, or indeed this book, without mentioning once again the special relationship that exists between children and angels. If you ever want a shot in the arm to believe in angels, ask children. They have the words, the ideas, the trust, the wonder and willingness to suspend disbelief and truly see and hear the miraculous. This is not the same as being innocent and naïve; it means not blanking out whatever does not conform to reason, logic and science. It means having an open mind and heart and the ability to feel things deeply and express them with-out fear, and it is this openness and emotional spontaneity that draws angels towards them.

I love asking children to tell me about angels. They always have so much to share and so much to say. I love how easily they accept and don't question their encounters. Often they talk about angels in a matter-of-fact way, and look at me as if I am the one who is in need of help if I don't understand, because in their minds nothing could be clearer and simpler. To children, there is no confusion and no doubt: angels are real.

This lovely story comes from Bev:

He's funny

I would like to share my story with you. My daughter Emma is three and a half now. The other day we'd all spent time in our garden, and after tea her daddy and I came in, but Emma wanted to play outside still. When I finally got her in and bathed, she told me something amazing.

I was lying on the sofa reading a book when she said to me, 'See him, he's funny, isn't he?' I asked her who she meant and she pointed to a photo of my grandpa Tom, who died ten years before so she had never met him. She then went on to say that when she was in the garden he had been talking to her and he'd made her laugh. I asked if she was sure, and she pointed again to his photo and was adamant that it was him.

And this enchanting one was sent to me by Dave.

Reaching up

I believe babies and children can see angels. When my son was old enough to babble he would always point at pictures of his grandfather whom he had never met and talk to him before bedtime. He would also fix his eyes on the ceiling and reach up and smile. My son in nearly five now, and recently before bedtime he starts waving to someone although there is only me and him in the room. The first time it happened, I asked him who he was waving at and he said, 'The angel lady dancing in the curtains.' The curtains in his bedroom have beautiful old-fashioned swirls on them and they were drawn. I asked him again who he was waving at and he said, 'The angel in the curtain.'

Now we both wave at the curtains before he goes to sleep. I have no doubt that he does see something there and that it is an angel. He is completely at ease with his angel lady and shows no fear whatsoever. It's not just in the curtains that my son sees angels – he tells me he also sees them in soap bubbles and in spider's webs and dewdrops. He is always so sincere and happy when he tells me that I have no choice but to believe in him and his magical world.

Magical stories like these remind us that angels can be found anywhere and everywhere, from curtain patterns to soap bubbles, from hugs to dewdrops, from rainbows to sunsets and in everything beautiful and magical. The presence of angels can be found in every glimmer of creation. They are part of the interaction behind all things visible and invisible, which children, and all those who have the heart of a child, can see.

Children can teach us a great deal about finding angels in our own lives. Their natural sense of wonder and open-mindedness is an open door for angels to enter. They are fresh from heaven, and 'grown-up' fear, scepticism and doubt haven't got there yet. They just know instinctively how to see the wonder in everyone and everything. Unfortunately, as we get older this ability to see a world of magic and possibility around us fades, but it doesn't have to be this way. We can all rediscover the child within us.

Remember, the child within us is the piece of us that longs to be loved and protected, however old we are. It is the piece of us that stays creative, intuitive, passionate, enthusiastic and wide-eyed, but it is also the piece of us most in need of guidance and reassurance. Many of us forget about our inner child, but it never disappears completely. At heart we are all children searching for magic and meaning, and it is through the innocent child in each of us that our guardian angel will speak to us.

There really is no need to look too far outside yourself to discover your angels. They are already within you, waiting to guide, help and protect you through your inner child.

Living in spirit

It is a sad fact that many children today are being pressured to grow up too fast and act like 'mini-adults' before they are ready. As technology has advanced, along the way our children are losing their imaginative powers, their willingness to suspend disbelief, their ability to feel a sense of awe and wonder for anyone or anything. We would all be playing our part in creating a more joyful, hopeful and magical future for our children if we encouraged them to learn more about angels and the magic they can bring to our lives. Of course, we all need to teach our children to be realistic and independent, but this doesn't mean that the price they must pay is leaving their creativity and sense of wonder behind.

And just as we should encourage our children to be imaginative, joyful and creative, we should also try to keep the spirit of our own childhood alive. We should let our fear, doubt and rigid thinking melt away, so that our hearts can open to the angels and then laughter, magic and love can flow back into our lives.

There is no reason in heaven or earth why you can't soar with the wondrous creative powers of your imagination. There is no reason why you can't believe in the impossible, or at the very least open your mind to it. There is no reason why you can't laugh, dance, sing or let your hair down if you feel like it. You are only as old as you think you are, and as long as you stay spontaneous, creative and loving, you will never grow old in the eyes of your angels.

Old age is a shadow that falls when you have forgotten how to love, but if you trust your angels you will never forget love nor will love forget you. Just reach out with the open and trusting heart of a child and there waiting to hold your hand will be your guardian angel ready to guide you, as a loving parent guides a child, through the challenges, opportunities and marvels that await you in this life and the next.

Living in spirit won't always be easy – if it was you would never learn and grow – but when you understand that however lost, alone or afraid you may feel an angel is always watching over you, it does become easier to deal with. This is the eternal promise your angels made to you when you were born, perhaps even before you were born. They will never leave you and are always there to help you realise your divine potential and become the amazing and powerful person they know you can be. They will never break their promise to you and the only thing you need to do in return is open your heart.

Allow yourself to be open to the messages from heaven being sent to you all the time. Their only aim is to make you feel safer and happier and to give your life more meaning. Your angels love you and more than anything else want you to find peace and contentment. Just ask for them and they will appear. And the more you ask them, the more you talk to them, the more magical your life will become.

Every time you let heaven help you, you don't just enrich your life, you enrich the lives of others because you reveal to them a glimpse of the divine on earth through your words, your actions and, above all, your newfound belief. So let the angel inside you speak to all people and watch your life become a series of divine encounters as a result. See the angel in everyone and everything and you will always be in divine company.

And by playing your part in making the world a brighter and a better place you will discover your destiny and your true meaning and a sense of real belonging. You will become part of the angels' promise to bring light, hope, peace and love to this world. And then when the moment comes for you to pass over to the other side, you will soar without dread or remorse to that higher place where there is only light, love, joy and peace.

You will soar heavenward.

Afterword:
When Heaven Speaks

You don't have to die to become an angel.

Author unknown

It's unlikely that we will ever be able to scientifically prove what happens when we die, since it's a bit like trying to prove a dream is true, but there is a way that we can catch a glimpse of the after-life and that is by studying near-death experiences, or NDEs.

There are at least fifteen million people around the world who have had what is known as a near-death experience, the experience of dying when the heart stops beating. It's not a topic generally discussed as many people feel uncomfortable talking about dying, but NDEs are real, and can tell us a great deal about life in spirit as well as life on earth. An honest study of NDEs can yield a wealth of information that has the capacity to dramatically change opinions and beliefs about what happens when we die.

Not everyone who experiences clinical death will have a NDE, and we don't know why, but for those that do report a NDE, although their experiences will all differ in details, there are always similar elements, regardless of their age, background, religion or culture. It's these similar elements that make NDEs perhaps the most compelling proof we have that life after death exists.

I'm summarising here, but typically those who have had a NDE report a feeling of calmness and detachment, followed by intense bright light that fills the room. The person may feel dissociated from their body in some way. Sometimes they can look down and see it, often describing the doctors working on it. Many then find themselves drawn to a tunnel filled with brilliant light. There may be angels or beings of light in that tunnel. They may encounter the spirit of a deceased loved one who may tell them it is not their time and that they need to go back to their body. There may also be a life review when the subject sees his or her entire life in flashback.

Usually when people have a NDE they realise that there are no words to describe what they experienced. Alice, whose story is below, talks about her experience as being more of a feeling and a sensation than something to describe in words.

Into the light

In 2002 I died for thirty-seven minutes. I had no pulse or blood flow and was shocked fourteen times before I came back. I had been driving to work and had this sharp pain in my chest. I just about managed to park and get out of my car but the pain kept increasing. I felt it down my left arm and in my chest. I knew I was having a heart attack. When a colleague found me semi-unconscious on the floor I was rushed to hospital and from then on I remember watching the scene unfold, as if from above.

Lying in hospital I floated right out of my body. It was as if I entered another dimension and I struggle to explain things here because we don't have words for that dimension. I did feel myself drawn to a dark valley or tunnel. I saw a brilliant light at the end of it and I had to get to the light. I didn't want to turn back. I saw deceased loved ones, including my dad and my ex-husband in that tunnel. Then I felt so peaceful, light and beautiful. I saw people I wouldn't have expected to see. I saw a friend from school I had lost touch with years ago. I saw myself picking up her books when she tripped over. I saw the boy who did our paper round ten years ago. I saw myself giving him some money to buy a pair of warm gloves. I saw the school bus driver who used to pick me up when I was a child. I saw myself offering him a sweet when he looked sad. I saw my driving instructor. I saw myself writing him a letter of gratitude for helping me pass my test first time round. Although these people hadn't touched my life in a dramatic way and I didn't really know them, I felt like I did. I wanted to reach out and hug them, but they floated away.

I felt myself getting closer and closer to the light. It wasn't a light, though. It felt like a person and that person was smiling at me. I laughed back. I felt like I was coming home. It was a glorious moment. Then I was overwhelmed by a massive energy, such a huge powerful energy. It was like how you feel when you fall in love, something so hard to describe to others. There aren't enough words to describe it and I can't give you the full picture. I do know that I understood everything that had happened in my life. Everything made sense. I saw pictures – colour photographs of my children and my granddaughter. The pictures triggered something in me. Things started to get confused again. The pictures stayed clear but nothing else was and then I came back into my body. I was conscious again, struggling to breathe on the operating table. I was alive but my heart was broken. I felt like I had left the love of my life behind.

I did make a full recovery. Doctors were astonished. I talked to them about what happened to me and they told me it was hallucination caused by a brain starved of oxygen. I didn't disagree. I didn't want them to think I was losing it, but I knew it was something much more profound than that. Two years later, although I didn't need proof, I sort of got it. A friend of a friend told me about one of the people I had seen in the afterlife – a person I didn't know very well but went to school with – she died ten years ago. I did some more research and all the people I saw, even that paper round boy, had died. I've moved area many times in my adult life and I would have had no idea they had passed over.

Something truly incredible happened to me when I died in hospital and it has changed the way I think about death for ever. It's also changed the way I think about life. I know it doesn't end. I have less pleasure now in material things and am more and more interested in things related to spirit.

As well as offering a spellbinding hint of what might await us all when we die, Alice's story also underlines a point I've been trying to make throughout this book, which is that everything we say and do in this life has an impact – even apparently trivial things or encounters we may forget along the way.

As was the case for Alice, after a NDE many people report a

dramatic change of attitude as a result. They see themselves and everyone and everything in a new light and live their lives in a more spiritual and thoughtful way. They also lose their fear of death. It is regrettable that so many of us today are so very frightened of death, but accounts like these – and I've researched and read hundreds in my time – show that we don't need to be afraid of death because life doesn't end with death. We can look forward to it as a new beginning. In this way NDEs can be a tremendous source of hope, comfort and encouragement.

Although near-death experiences usually occur when a person is in danger of losing their life, you don't actually need to 'die' to discover life in spirit. Indeed, until now I deliberately steered clear of including NDEs in this book, because as powerful and compelling evidence as they may be for life in spirit, I wanted to make the point that you don't need to be close to death, or in a life-or-death situation, to see or hear angels. You can encounter them in every aspect of normal life.

While it is true that suffering and crisis can foster spiritual growth, it is equally true that peace and contentment create more. You can learn even more through peace and through love, through stillness and silence. You don't need to float out of your body to become a more spiritual person or see the light. You can be the light. You don't need to encounter the spirits of departed loved ones to hear the voices of angels. You can hear them now in moments of quiet reflection. You don't need to enter a tunnel of light to know that death is not the end but a beginning. You don't need to wait for that shock. You can enter a new life in love, peace and spirit right here, right now.

In much the same way, you don't need to wait for a full-blown angel vision or encounter to catch a glimpse of heaven on earth. You can glimpse its wonder right now inside your heart. All the answers you have been seeking can be found there, and when you start to understand and experience angels in this way, from the inside out, you will start to have the most incredible feelings of love and hope gathering apace inside you. Instead of feeling uncomfortable in times of silence and solitude you will feel surrounded by warmth and light. This isn't to say that all your problems will disappear, but you will be filled with a newfound sense of purpose and meaning that gives you the strength to cope with anything life throws at you.

As you've seen many times in this book, angels are more likely to speak to you in subtle, soft ways, gently nudging you in the right direction with uplifting thoughts and feelings from within. Many people don't realise that they prefer you to discover them in this quiet, wordless way, because this is the most powerful and true way for you to connect with them. Your real self can never be found on the surface of life. You have to look deep inside yourself for all that you need to be the divine, caring, perfect, beautiful, powerful and wonderful part of you – your inner angel.

Remember in this life you can already be an angel. If you welcome your day with an open heart, your memories and your diary are full of angel experiences already. If you can live your life with courage, heart and compassion, you will be given the right words to speak with, a healed heart to love with and a deep sense of your own truth. If you give yourself moments of truth and silence, you will rediscover the angel inside you and others will see something light and inspirational in you. Then one day very soon, when you least expect it, the voice with which heaven speaks to everyone will be yours.

It is a time for angels to reveal themselves on earth, beginning with you. Begin to be an angel for you and then for the people around you. Begin now and you help hundreds. Everything we say and do in this life has the power to touch others in a divine way. A single smile can brighten a person's day, a kind and gentle word can help someone feel positive about life again, a selfless caring deed can bring a ray of sunshine into the lives of others, and a loving and compassionate heart can draw the angels nearer to earth, bringing with them their pure goodness and light.

As reflections of your own divine potential your angels speak to the deepest and mightiest part of yourself, the part of yourself that can move mountains and bring heaven down to earth. When you are not listening to the angel inside you, you are not being yourself and your angels won't be able to speak to you.

You probably began reading this book thinking you might learn something new, but the truth is you were just remembering something you already knew; something your spirit has already heard. You are not alone. Your angels are all around and within you. You can hear them speaking to you anytime you want when you pause to reflect in peace and silence, and listen to the beating of your own heart. You are not searching for truth, love and light. You *are* truth, love and light, and when you remember this, you will 'just know' that you can never end – you are eternal.

An angel is born every moment, let the next one be you.

I'll finish, for now, with a couple of angelic quotes to guide and inspire you and, as always, my favourite angel blessing to reassure and remind you.

Go placidly amid the noise and haste and remember what peace there is in silence.

Desiderata

The greatest achievement was at first and for a time a dream. The oak sleeps in the acorn, the bird waits in the egg, and in the highest vision of the soul a waking angel stirs. Dreams are the seedlings of realities.

James Allen

Angel Blessing

Angels around us, angels beside us, angels within us. Angels are watching over you when times are good or stressed. Their wings wrap gently around you, whispering you are loved and blessed.

About the Author

Theresa Cheung is the author of a variety of books including the *Sunday Times* bestsellers *An Angel Called My Name, An Angel on My Shoulder* and *Angel Babies.* She is also the author of the international bestseller *The Element Encyclopedia of 20,000 Dreams,* and *The Element Encyclopedia of the Psychic World* and the recent top ten Sunday Times bestseller *An Angel Healed Me* as well as *An Angel Changed My Life* and *How to See Your Angels.*

Theresa's books have been translated into twenty different languages and her writing has featured in *Chat – It's Fate, Spirit & Destiny, Prediction, Red* and *Prima* magazines, as well as the *Daily Express, Daily Mail* and *Sunday Times Style.* In addition, Theresa has worked on books for Derek Acorah, Yvette Fielding, Tony Stockwell and Dr William Bloom. Born into a family of psychics and spiritualists, Theresa has been involved in the research of psychic phenomena for over twenty-five years since gaining a Masters from King's College, Cambridge. She has also been a student at the College of Psychic Studies in London.

Calling All Angels

If you have an angel story, experience or insight and wish to share it with Theresa, she would love to hear from you. Please contact her care of Simon and Schuster, 1st Floor, 222 Gray's Inn Road, London WC1X 8HB or email her at: angeltalk710@aol.com